THE INEVITABLE
RISE
OF THE
SHERO NATION

DR. BARBARA
WALKER GREEN

I

Paperback ISBN: 978-1-7354642-2-0

Book Project Managed by McWriting Services, in the United States of America.

First printing, 2020.

McWriting Services

2162 Spring Stuebner Rd
Suite#140-1018
Spring, TX 77389
www.mcwritingservices.com

Cover Photo by Ferrell Phelps of Ferrells Photography

TABLE OF CONTENTS

Acknowledgements... V

Foreword VII

Introduction 1

CHAPTER I
Theories that Bind...7

CHAPTER II
The Trap...27

CHAPTER III
The Glass Cliff Theory 39

CHAPTER IV
A Shero Defined..53

CHAPTER V
Sheroes: Past, Present,
and Future...67

CHAPTER VI
Asunder..93

CHAPTER VII
The Shero Within 113

About The Author 125

ACKNOWLEDGEMENTS

A sincere and deep acknowledgement goes to those who are in my life who have made a difference in my life in ways maybe even they do not know. I would like to first acknowledge my mom. My mom is my shero, my number one shero! As the mother of seven, she loves us unconditionally and shows us what it means to be a family that loves each other and helps each other even when it hurts. I acknowledge my children, Shaolin and Julian Walker. We have a family mantra we call "three-deep." Three deep signifies that we must focus on passing pillars of wealth three-generations deep. At this time, I have no grandchildren, but when I do, it is my duty to pass wealth to my children's children. We are not finished until we have passed enough wealth – and not just monetary, but the wealth of traditions, self-reflection, and the knowledge of how to be the best that you can be, and the wealth of knowing your history and defining your purpose in this life. This message must be actively and deliberately passed down three-generations deep. I actively participate in passing these pillars of wealth to my children and ultimately to my great grandchildren at the very least. I pray that I am able to live to pass these pillars in a way that transcends generational differences

I acknowledge my sisters and brothers: Rosetta, Carolyn, Robert, Sharon, Johnnie, and Kenny. Without them in my life, I would not be who I am. Each and every one of them touches me in a different way just as I do them. We are strong; we are united, and that is what has made us all so special to each other. We see each other as sisters and brothers; that is it. Though our brother, Johnnie is not here with us physically, he is a daily part of our lives spiritually. As our brother Robert lay resting in a convalescent hospital, our love for him remains as strong as ever. I acknowledge you all. I love you all.

I acknowledge Charles Bowie. Charles is a man that gives 110% of himself, from his heart and soul. He is there for me. He loves me, and I acknowledge him. I love you, Charles.

I give special acknowledgment to my recently deceased doctoral chairperson, Dr. Kriesta Watson. Dr. Kri, I listened to you! I hope to make you proud. Without your words of conviction, I would not be on this journey today. Rest in peace, dear friend.

To Sharon C. Jenkins of Mc Writing Services and Dr. Shannicka Johnson of LIGHT in Education, thank you for walking with me through this labor of love. Your wisdom, expertise, and guidance of helping me to curate and capture the journey and evolution of the shero has been priceless. Like me, you have lived much of this journey and can attest to its value and importance. I am thankful beyond measure for both of you. You are true sheroes!

Finally, I acknowledge those in my life who mean so much to me – my friends, my colleagues, my clients, those who work alongside me, and those who encourage me. There are so many of you out there. You all know who you are, and I love each of you.

FOREWORD

There comes a time in a woman's life when she is faced with the very real choice of publicly proclaiming who she is, what she believes in and how she will make her voice heard. Her appointed time at this declaration is undeniable and the sheer evolutionary process is remarkable to witness. I call this period in a woman's life her moment of rising and Dr. Barbara Walker-Green has done a remarkable job at describing this process in her brilliant book The Inevitable Rise of Shero Nation.

As you read through the pages of this book you'll be inspired by the stories, enlightened by Dr. Walker Green's research and supplemental findings, moved by her transparency and honesty, and encouraged to take bold and swift action as a woman who is rising in the Shero Nation.

Conversely, Dr. Walker-Green takes no prisoners and uncovers the stark inequities and inadequacies women face. She guides us on how to better understand gender-based bias and the traps, prejudice, stereotypes, unfair treatment, misogyny, and the myriad of challenges that women face and continue to fight against.

For some readers, like myself, this may be your first introduction to the concepts of The Bourdieusian Framework, Double Binds and the Glass Cliff Theory. I'm now fascinated by the explanations and applications that Dr. Walker-Green provides in this book.

I find all of this to be enlightening, educational and motivational. As a two-time Emmy award winning TV Host, Veteran TV news anchor, TEDx presenter, author, award winning filmmaker, and life and business coach, I've spent my entire life recognizing and honoring powerful women like Dr. Walker Green. It's been my pleasure and honor to tell their stories, produce their works of art and coach them to higher levels of visibility and success.

I know personally what a distinct recognition it is to be considered a shero, earning the right to consider myself within a class of women who have displayed courage, bravery, resolve, fortitude and faith.

I am a survivor of cybersexual rape and assault, harassment, stalking, and extortion.

I was cyber-stalked and cyber raped by an ex-boyfriend, who put up a website with damaging and harassing memes and nude photos and videos of me that he had been secretly taking of me.

After months of isolation, suffering in shame and silence, I rose from this very humiliating, painful and potentially professionally damaging incident.

I've created a global movement called 50 Shades of Silence, to bring voice and dignity to victims of cyber harassment and online crimes. Specifically, 50 Shades of Silence aims to advocate for stricter laws and tougher enforcement for cyber sexual crimes, encourage the accountability and responsiveness among online companies, promote social responsibility for texting, posting and sharing online, and restore dignity and respect to victims and survivors.

While I didn't know Dr. Walker Green during my darkest days and I didn't have The Inevitable Rise of Shero Nation in my hands and at my disposal, I trust, had I, I would have been able to traverse the very confusing and painful period in my life with the knowledge that I am not alone. I would have been able to be encouraged by Dr. Walker Green's insight into the character and prowess of a woman who calls herself a Shero. I would have simply been given the tools to Rise faster, stronger, easily and more confident. I am now a proud Shero who knows very intimately what it means to rise.

Fortunately, you now have this rich resource at your disposal. You will now know as you turn the pages of this book, how to traverse the many obstacles you will be faced with. Read it with care, embrace it with an open mind, use it as an instrument to spread the message of women's empowerment. There are endless possibilities and so many options for a better future and tomorrow for young girls and women.

You could be in no better hands or for that matter have no better book in your hands to help you and others rise and be a proud woman in this Shero Nation.

Darieth Chisolm

Introduction

My name is Dr. Barbara Walker-Green. I am a shero. Right now, you might question who is a shero and what is her makeup. I wrote this book to answer those questions. I also wrote this book to be a safe place for women and men to learn, appreciate, and most of all become active participants in what happens going forward. A life awakening is yours to experience after reading this book if you take stock in its evidence.

I invite every reader to be empowered. Today is the day that you begin your realization; you will be pushed to acknowledge *The Inevitable Rise of the Shero Nation*. Within these pages, you will encounter not only "ah-ha" moments and epiphanies, but most importantly, you will find permission to unify, support, and engage with one another on the subject of women's equality. You will understand that the evolution is not a negative thing but a reality of life. Just as humankind evolves, so have women in our shero evolution.

I wrote this book for women to use as a magnifying glass to take a glimpse at the origin of exactly what holds us back, challenges us, and identify those blind spots that we often run into. I hope that women will see clearly how and where invisible enemies come from and be able to navigate through their trajectory. Each chapter in this book serves as part of the navigation gear.

Chapter One is an introduction to theories that bind women socially, culturally, and as the female gender. Perhaps these theories came about innocently, but no doubt we continue to live with and feel their effects today. The lessons to be learned regarding theories that bind are lesson beneficial to all.

Chapter Two discusses traps and how the fiery theories explained in Chapter 1 influences societal expectations and pre-dispositions on women that are physical and mental traps. I discuss how the traps of the theories that bind acts as a self-fulfilling prophecy because women continuously fight against binding social and cultural expectations.

Chapter Three delves into a theory that has been studied by scholars for many years. It is rooted in real-life situations where women are placed in leadership positions with the full expectation of failure. This theory is not well acknowledged by men, but women who are familiar with the theory fully acknowledge its existence.

Chapter Four explores who the shero is, how she is identified, and how powerful she is in her own right. I introduce concepts such as habitus, capital, and the double edge of narcissistic traits.

Chapter Five acts as a guide along the road of discovery from the beginnings of the shero movement to present times. I cover the road to progress from our late sheroes, and baby-boomer sheroes, to our millennial sheroes. Along the way, roadblocks, detours, and yes, the effect of the technological revolution is made obvious and how technology tosses bitter-sweet road blocks in our path.

Chapter Six, the most powerful of the chapters, speaks to how sheroes are here and now – strong and gaining strength in such a way that nothing and no one can break it into parts or dis-unite it. Yes, this chapter, "Asunder," originates from the scripture "...let no man put asunder" and is meant to imply that the rise of the Shero Nation is ordained by God and therefore cannot be stopped.

Chapter Seven visits my personal evolution and ties some of my experiences to all the elements discussed in the previous chapters as a point of self-reflection. Find yourself in the words on these pages. Use this time to reflect on how these elements may be present in your own life and how you can use this new information to your advantage.

My inspiration for writing this book came from a place within where my life's lessons reside – the storage place of my soul where my trials, successes, and failures reside, but mostly my life's battles fighting against invisible foes.

My very soul gave birth to this book, *The Inevitable Rise of the Shero Nation*. As a daughter, sister, and mother, I long for each woman to achieve and flourish in her own success where no man, no theory, or no culture beliefs inhibit her growth. I relish in the fact that we rise; we are rising, and we will continue to rise. I pray that one day as sheroes unite we can all stand as one and support one another, not that we have to agree or understand, but just to support each other, for united we stand, and divided we shall surely fall.

I hold dear the lessons learned and the messages that I send out into the world through the writing of this book. As we continue to come into our own, we will reach a time and place where we are undeniable, and we can take our rightful place in this country and in the world!

MARY CHAN
PODCASTER - MOM

My podcast adventure started way back in radio. After a 20-year career in radio, I got downsized. I realized I loved listening to podcasts but noticed some of the ones I listened to didn't sound that great and I figured I have this audio editing skillset – I could help people create better sounding podcasts. So, in 2018, I started my company "Organized Sound Productions". From there I launched a show with a good friend of mine and now I've been helping a whole bunch of organizations and independent podcasters create their show.

In thinking about the future… I find that right now there aren't enough women podcasting. It's definitely grown in the last year, but women will find that they can use this platform as a way to embody their voice. There are a lot of bloggers who are women, but words are only one aspect of communication. The stat is that 7% of communication is words, the rest of it has to do with your body language or tone. Tone is actually 38% of communication so you can really increase that connection and intimacy with people - your listeners, your audience-- through your voice and tone using podcasting. People are just realizing that now, and it's just the tip of the iceberg-- especially if you are going to be using your podcast as a business owner. If you are a CEO, you should have a podcast so that people get to know who you are. I think we are going to see a massive spike and massive growth for women using podcasting.

For me, using this platform, I hope to inspire other women to enter this industry. I want to show them that it can be done by anyone who might look the way you look or speak the way you speak-- with stumbles and ums and speech impediments or an accent. You still have a valid message to share and that's what I want to get across. It's never too early to start!

ABOUT HER DAUGHTER

I am equipping my daughter to own her power. Even before she was 1 year old, I realized she understood what I was saying and was reacting to what I was saying before she had words of her own. One example was I was too lazy to get off the couch and she was playing in the corner and she had some books, and I said "Oh, if you bring the purple one over to me I'll read it to you" and she looked at me and saw the two books, she picked up the pink one and I was like "oh no, that's the pink one I mean the other one, the purple one" and she showed it to me and I said "YES! Come over here." She didn't say a word, didn't have any words and that's when I realized "oh my gosh she is already absorbing everything that I'm telling her." So right then and there I started talking to her about starting daycare the next month and saying "you might look different from other people but that's going to be OK. Because being unique is great, being different is great. Everybody should be different and share their differences." Now she is 4 turning 5 and struggling with playing with other kids because she doesn't want other kids to break her toys, so I say "well, you have a voice – use your voice, what do you want to say?" "Well I don't want them to break my toys" "Alright so how can we say that nicely? How about: This toy is very important to me; can we play with a different toy? And just make sure that you also don't hurt other people's feelings". I help her choose the right words and always make sure that she uses her voice in some capacity, especially as a girl. It is very important for me to let her know that her feelings are valid, and she should express them.

I don't want to shy away from speaking to her about the future. She is a person, not just a child, she's not a baby. She should know what is going on in the world. Yes, maybe bringing it down to her level, but teaching her the happenings in the world in that moment so that she can take that now and translate it into whatever future she wants to create for herself because I can't do that for her. She still has to make those choices, so I want to equip her with as much knowledge as I can now so she can make the right decisions when it is her time.

CHAPTER I

Theories that Bind

As a driven African-American woman, the natural progression of my professional track was to pursue a doctorate degree. My doctoral journey changed my perspective on life. Alongside me on this journey was my assigned mentor and chairperson, a brilliant young woman by the name of Doctor Kriesta Watson. Dr. Watson made a major impression on my life. She was 13 years my junior. At that time, however, she saw in me what I did not see for myself. One day she said three words to me that changed the direction of my thinking: "Barbara, it's your time." Those three words were plain and simple. "It's [my] time." After decades of working hard in the corporate world and ultimately starting my own financial practice, "it's my time" hit me like a quick burst of air. It was enough to startle me but not enough to move me until she died suddenly at the young age of 46. This brilliant, confident, and poised woman was gone. Her death made me rethink what she said to me.

If it really was "my time," was I taking full advantage of it? If not, what held me captive in a place that should have only been a stepping stone towards greater things? Why had I not processed the power of that moment immediately and been challenged enough to seek out what a possible adventure would look like? I believe this chapter will answer those questions and bring clarity to norms, systems, and theories that tend to bind us.

Throughout this book I describe our journey as women – one of strength and resilience necessary to resist barriers that have evaded time. I provide research and historical accounts to acknowledge these obstacles, so our discussion will sound a bit technical at times. By the same token, I share intimate experiences and commentary regarding women who have and continue navigating and conquering these challenges. Their harnessed strength and perseverance resulted in notable accomplishments for them, those aspiring to rise as leaders after them, and those populating a great rising nation of women. As a member of this rising nation, I am sure you will find this discussion relatable. I invite you to walk with me through this transformation of mindsets, circumstances, and individual growth. For now, we will begin with theories that bind, as they remain the core of our inhibitions regarding leadership.

Being hindered is nothing new for women. For hundreds of years, we have been under societal limitations as well as skepticism about our talents and true worth. Since the days of our founding father, John Adams, women have fought the good fight to be recognized as equal in the citizenry of the United States. In the awakening and birth of a new nation, Abigail Adams wrote the following to her husband, John, and members of the Continental Congress March 31, 1776:

> *I long to hear that you have declared an independency - and by the way, in the new code of laws which I suppose it will be necessary for you to make, I desire you would remember the ladies and be more generous and favorable to them than your ancestors. Do not put such unlimited power into the hands of the husbands. Remember, all men would be tyrants if they could. If particular care and attention is not paid to the ladies, we are determined to foment a rebellion, and will not hold ourselves bound by any laws in which we have no voice or representation.* [1]

Abigail Adams penned these words almost 150 years before approval of the 19th Amendment, which gave women the right to vote. Her words challenged the status quo because they urged her husband and his colleagues to prioritize the rights of women. Moreover, her words alluded to invisible barriers women faced. These persistent barriers transcended time and continue to act as binding agents that allow gender bias to continue to flourish. Since women's right to vote did not happen until over 100 years

---

1. "Abigail Adams to John Adams, 31 March 1776," Founders Online, National Archives, https://founders.archives.gov/documents/Adams/04-01-02-0241.

after she wrote these words, it is obvious that her sentiments were met with resistance. I am sure a current level of resistance would still challenge Abigail Adams' passionate position. Ingrained within that resistance lies a myriad of mindsets influenced by theories, systems, and norms permeating our society today.

Reflecting on history helped me to realize what held me captive is not just one thing; it is a conglomerate of traditions and attitudes used to shape widely-accepted theories, norms, and systems. I deepen my reflection in this chapter by examining theories that bind the mindset of women and society as a whole. This chapter speaks to ingrained ideals that grip the very movement of women in society today. As women, we have faced viewpoints from society since the beginning of time that put us at a disadvantage in many cases, particularly when it comes to deciding our path and blazing our own trail. Most social theories in Western culture directly affect how we pattern and move through our own personal journeys. Examining theories that bind will help clear a path for us to push aside old belief systems and clear the road for a smoother ride along the way.

Theories that Bind

The journey we are about to take through the pages of this book will include a whirlwind of concepts not common to most. These concepts will set the stage for understanding the challenges that women have faced and continue to face from a not so familiar perspective. We will take a walk along the path that women before us walked while shining a bright light on the hidden forces directly affecting the movement of women in society.

The shero concept speaks to the "she-hero" that women evolve into as we fight for our basic and human rights.

Note the underlying conflict. Hidden forces acting against women's forward movement. Women making progressive steps in spite of those hidden forces are sheroes. The shero concept speaks to the "she-hero" that women evolve into as we fight for our basic and human rights. The shero profile will be fully defined and discussed in Chapter 4 but, for now, we will delve into the hidden shackles that have bound women throughout history – socially accepted and ingrained theories.

Clearly, we as women possess the potential and skill set to effectively lead in a variety of ways. Numerous barriers that limit our opportunities to do so are not so clear. Though not easily detected by the naked eye, the following three theories, Role Congruity Theory, Social Role Theory, and Glass Cliff Theory, are prevalent in American society and hinder our progress into the upper echelons of leadership in America and around the world. I discuss each theory in this chapter and explain norms and structures that influence all of them.

Role Congruity Theory

Role Congruity Theory explains the grossly unequal number of women in top-level management.[2] The foundation of this theory is based on a perceived incongruity between the attributes of strong leaders and attributes assigned by social norms to women's gender roles. This theory proposes a perceived incongruity between male and female leadership ability leading to gender-biased prejudices.[3] These prejudices include the perception that women are less effective than men in leadership roles. Evidence confirms that these consequences occur, particularly in situations that heighten perceptions of incongruity between female gender roles and leadership roles related to executive appointments in the corporate and political culture.[4]

Society often ponders comparison questions such as, "Who makes more competent leaders, men or women? Are men better than women at leading? Can women step up to the [leadership] plate?" Unfortunately, questions like these have a nuance—a bias against us, women. The Role Congruity Theory explains the root cause behind this type of inquiry while uncovering inconspicuous tones of partiality for our male counterparts. This theory uses widely-accepted gender roles to compare our leadership to that of men. It begins to explain the "why" behind a doubting mindset regarding our abilities to lead. It also sheds insight to the lagging representation of women in leadership roles.

2. Alice H. Eagly and Steven J. Karau. "Role Congruity Theory of Prejudice toward Female Leaders." Psychological Review 109, no. 3 (2002): 573–98. https://doi.org/10.1037/0033-295x.109.3.573.
3. Eagly and Karau, 573.
4. Eagly and Karau, 589.

Simply put, Role Congruity Theory, implies that women and power do not go together. This theory, designed and manufactured by men, has bound women in positions of less income for the same work, the expectation of a greater share of household duties, and in some cases, blatant acts against us including verbal and physical violence (femicide). Theories of incongruity are ingrained in the mindsets of people and are difficult to change in the short run. As I examine this theory and unpack its contents, think along with me so that we can destroy its power.

Social Role Theory

Social Role Theory is based on the principle that men and women behave differently in social situations and should take on the roles that are socially acceptable for their respective genders.[5]

These expectations, a form of gender stereotyping, dictates what society sees as suitable behaviors for men versus what is suitable for women. This includes women taking positions of lower power, having a bulk of the responsibility for the domestic tasks in relationships, and the idea that men and women have different occupational roles based on their psychological and physiological characteristics.

Social Role Theory contends that all psychological differences can be attributed to expectations of gender and cultural standards rather than biological factors.[6] It builds on the think-manager-think-male framework.[7] This psychological phenomenon is very well-known and exists because the traits we typically associate with leaders – forceful, dominant, strong, competent or even heroic – are stereotypically associated with men. This framework analyzes the role of male leadership and dominates leadership literature.[8]

In the late 1970's, psychologist Virginia Schein completed a series of experiments which indicated that both male and female managers viewed

5. Eagly and Karau.
6. Eagly and Karau, 568-570.
7. Andrea Fischbach, Philipp W. Lichtenthaler, and Nina Horstmann. "Leadership and Gender Stereotyping of Emotions." Journal of Personnel Psychology 14, no. 3 (2015): 153–62. https://doi.org/10.1027/1866-5888/a000136.
8. Fischbach et al., 152.

management positions as masculine and better fitted for males.[9] These indications reflect the culture and socio-economic status of women during the early 1970s. Contemporary authors argue that responses from female managers starting in the 20th century no longer hold such stereotypical views. Reactions from female managers in later studies reveal women's contention that both male and female managers possess traits that can make them successful leaders. The change in thinking is attributed to the view of leadership roles among women and changes in social functions. In the early 20th century, women began to aggressively challenge men in the labor force which evoked a change in the viewpoint regarding women and leadership. However, the shift in viewpoints is not the result of a change in the male perspective.[10] Gender-biased perceptions of female leadership ability continue to be prominent within leadership theory.

Social Role Theory says to society that women should "stay in their lane."

Like Role Congruity Theory, Social Role Theory is grounded in gender bias and stereotypes. Because we live in a climate of male dominance in leadership, this theory assumes that characteristics associated with male leadership reign supreme to those widely-accepted for females. It further explains the restrictive mindset women leaders and their aspiring protégés encounter.

Social Role Theory says to society that women should "stay in their lane." As women, we must first be cognizant of where this attitude comes from so that we can redirect its power towards mending gender inequities.

Glass Cliff Theory

The Glass Cliff Theory refers to the phenomenon whereby women are more likely than men to be appointed to leadership positions in times when they are expected to fail.[11] As a result, these women are more subject to criticism because these positions involve leading during a time of crisis.

9. Virginia E. Schein. "Sex Role Stereotyping, Ability and Performance: Prior Research and New Directions." Personnel Psychology 31, no. 2 (1978): 259–68. https://doi.org/10.1111/j.1744-6570.1978.tb00445.x.

10 Meghna Sabharwal. "From Glass Ceiling to Glass Cliff: Women in Senior Executive Service." Journal of Public Administration Research and Theory 25, no. 2 (2013): 399–426. https://doi.org/10.1093/jopart/mut030.

11 Terrance W. Fitzsimmons and Victor J. Callan. "Applying a Capital Perspective to Explain Continued Gender Inequality in the C-Suite." The Leadership Quarterly 27, no. 3 (2016): 354–70. https://doi.org/10.1016/j.leaqua.2015.11.003.

This phenomenon holds that women are promoted to senior roles due to societal perceptions of the leadership attributes they bring to a crisis situation.[12] Women are perceived as better equipped to handle conflict because society deems their leadership style as more nurturing.[13] The gender biases inherent in this theory contain inequities in the workplace including workload, sexism, lack of access to social networks, and other direct and indirect forms of discrimination and bias.[14] The Glass Cliff Theory aids in the examination of the interaction between societal perceptions and organizational factors that undermine women's successful attainment of positions in leadership.

The Glass Cliff Theory operates under the guise of "appropriately" promoting women to effectively lead the way during intensely difficult and critical situations.

Finally, a theory that recognizes the positive attributes of women leaders, right? Not necessarily. The Glass Cliff Theory operates under the guise of "appropriately" promoting women to effectively lead the way during intensely difficult and critical situations. Some people may think of it as an opportunity for women to successfully lead against the odds. That may be the intent in some cases. The reality in most cases, however, is that women in these positions have been set up with the expectation to fail. The Glass Cliff Theory pays special attention to failure of women in senior ranking positions.[15]

Role Congruity, Social Role, and Glass Cliff theories help us to better understand how male dominance influences social constructs that act as barriers for women's leadership in Western culture. Now that the three theories have been explained, we will explore a bit deeper by looking at social norms and systems built upon these three theories.

Perceptions Regarding Emotion and Leadership Ability

The accepted norm that women are overtly more emotional than men is one of the most influential gender stereotypes in Western cultures. As leaders, women

---

12. Fitzsimmons and Callan, 358.
13. See note 12.
14. Fitzsimmons and Callan, 360.
15. Sabharwal.

must walk a tightrope to maintain the perception of power. Brescoll (2016) researched the tightrope of emotion and described how women's expression of emotion presents a fundamental barrier to their ability to ascend to and succeed as leaders.[16] The study explains the nature of gender-emotion stereotypes. Examination of this research reveals that society has gendered-beliefs that women are more emotional than men.[17] However, Brescoll's meta-analysis results showed that men and women do not differ substantially to the extent of which they experience emotion, just in the degree to which they outwardly express emotions to others. Women are subjected to different rules, labeled as unable to control the outward display of emotion, and viewed as less capable of controlling how emotions influence them.[18]

Interestingly, Brescoll's study suggests that "the lay belief that emotion introduces irrational biases into decision-making processes is unfounded."[19] The consequence of this biased belief depicts women as ineffective leaders. Society views women's decision-making behaviors as influenced by emotion and therefore irrational, lacking objectivity, biased, unstable, unpredictable, and sentimental.[20] Gender stereotypes of emotion present obstacles to our ability as women to effectively lead others. The stereotype of emotion and its relationship to gender-biased perceptions of women's leadership ability attempts to hinder the growth in the number of women reaching upper echelons of leadership.

The olden perspective deemed inside of the home as the best place for women's "emotional" leadership.

The olden perspective deemed inside of the home as the best place for women's "emotional" leadership. Thus, it made sense for women to provide emotional support that structured and stabilized the home. Their historical roles as nurturing caretakers shaped the division of labor within the family unit, and it became the norm for women to take care of the home. However, fulfillment of these roles morphed into a hindrance for modern-day women like us who pursue leadership opportunities outside of our homes.

---

16. Victoria L. Brescoll. "Leading with Their Hearts? How Gender Stereotypes of Emotion Lead to Biased Evaluations of Female Leaders." The Leadership Quarterly 27, no. 3 (2016): 415–28. https://doi.org/10.1016/j.leaqua.2016.02.005.

17. Brescoll, 427.

18. See note 17.

19. Brescoll, 418.

20. See note 19.

Though it is considered an archaic practice by some, the division of labor in the family continues to impede our access to leadership positions. Numerous studies show that the number of children has the most substantial marginal effect on the likelihood of women becoming CEOs.[21] As a result, we as women step out of our careers to take care of children and family more often than men. This is consistent with findings that the division of labor within the family continues to have a high degree of influence on our appointments to high-level positions.

Norms of Male Organizational Culture

Think about the basic definition for male organizational culture. Male organizational culture reflects the values, beliefs, and norms that characterize an organization with a heavily male-dominated population.[22] This definition suggests that organizational culture reflects what is common, typical, and general for the organization. According to academic studies, the obstacle to equal representation of women revolves around male models of leadership and norms of male organizational culture.[23] This model appreciates agentic traits such as ambition, competitiveness, aggression, and control which are culturally assigned to men. On the other hand, there is less appreciation for more communal traits such as empathy, kindness, or concern for others, as these traits are considered "feminine." Society considers senior management positions as "masculine." This gender-biased consideration is responsible for the broad imbalance of women in senior executive-level positions.

As we attain senior-level leadership positions, we feel forced to adopt more "masculine" qualities to bypass this obstacle. In the absence of a suitable mechanism that would enable us to combine career and family optimally, male organizational culture presents an additional barrier whereby we must make concessions in our family makeup. The unequal standard of higher expectations remains elusive for our respective male counterparts. Not only

21. Brescoll, 416.
22. Fitzsimmons and Callan.
23. Fitzsimmons and Callan; Avigail Moor, Ayala Cohen, and Ortal Beeri. "In Quest of Excellence, Not Power: Women's Paths to Positions of Influence and Leadership." Advancing Women in Leadership 35, no. 1 (2014): 1-11. https://search.proquest.com/openview/932389c9e1615aa6b940938ecabaaef9/1?pq-origsite=gscholar&cbl=44345.

must we walk and talk as confident and competent individuals in our specific areas, but we must also understand and assimilate to a norm unnatural for who we are. This is how we attain and maintain higher ranks in government and corporate America. Clearly, this is above and beyond what men are expected to do within the comfort of the male-dominated climate.

The Old Boy Network

The "old boy network" is an informal male social system present in organizations. It purposely excludes less-dominant men and women from membership to ban together and preserve the upper ranks as a predominantly male domain.[24] This informal social system originates in early childhood experiences for boys and can be partially explained by the Bourdieusian framework. Fitzsimmons and Callan applied the Bourdieusian framework to their examination of the appointment of men and women to executive leadership positions.[25] Application of the framework deepens the understanding of how childhood experiences influence disparities between the genders subsequently impacting men and women's leadership preparation and success.

The different treatment of boys and girls around taking risks in childhood play promotes less self-confidence and self-esteem for women later in work.

Among other things, the Bourdieusian framework examines the cause of inter-generational gender disparity in social settings. Pierre Bourdieu, the author of the framework, explains that early childhood and adolescence is the peak time for developing gendered behavior passively acquired by observing societal norms.[26] Bourdieu's framework also reports that each gender acquires behavioral tendencies appropriate to the gender roles they observe during early childhood. As evidence of this, early life influences the parental division of labor can determine role occupancy later in life. Societal-level effects create gendered contexts for capital creation in

24. Judith G. Oakley. "Gender-based Barriers to Senior Management Positions: Understanding the Scarcity of Female CEOs." Journal of Business Ethics 27, no. 4 (2000): 321–34. https://doi.org/10.1023/a:1006226129868.
25. Fitzsimmons and Callan, 355.
26. Fitzsimmons and Callan, 357.
27. Fitzsimmons and Callan, 358.

children.[27] For example, some contexts in childhood offer boys the ability to take risks, act independently, and be successful. These outcomes promote self-confidence in males around risk-taking later in life. The different treatment of boys and girls around taking risks in childhood play promotes less self-confidence and self-esteem for women later in work.[28] Shyness is more socially acceptable for female children, but reinforcing this behavior happens at the expense of self-confidence and assertive behaviors.[29]

Additionally, games that boys traditionally play, such as football and other full contact team sports, contribute to the development of "resilience, leadership, strategic thinking, and an understanding of the importance of social capital."[30] This framework considers learned capabilities as valuable capital. Embodied understanding is more than merely conceptual understanding; rather, it encompasses our most basic way of being in, and engaging with our surroundings in a profound visceral manner.[31] Bourdieu defines capital as "all goods, material and symbolic, without distinction, that present themselves as rare and worthy of being sought after in a particular social formation."[32] This capital is attained through life experiences and social expectations that shape roles and behaviors towards each gender group.[33] Interestingly, the Bourdieusian framework describes how this valuable capital allows for the domination of one group of individuals, namely male leaders, to intergenerationally reproduce views about useful capital without widespread resistance.[34] These individuals can designate what valuable capital is required and the preferred context in which it is generated. In male-dominated executive and CEO roles, powers that preclude women from obtaining valuable combinations of capital are primarily responsible for the unequal representation of women reaching executive status. Fitzsimmons and Callan's 2016 examination using the Bourdieusian framework supports the premise that gendered patterns in the accumulation of career-relevant experiences stretch back to birth. These gender-related

---

28. Barbara White, Charles Cox, and Cary L. Cooper. Women's Career Development: A Study of High Flyers. Oxford: Blackwell Publishing, 1992.
29. Laura Doey, Robert J. Coplan, and Mila Kingsbury. "Bashful Boys and Coy Girls: A Review of Gender Differences in Childhood Shyness." Sex Roles 70, no. 7-8 (2013): 255–66. https://doi.org/10.1007/s11199-013-0317-9.
30. Fitzsimmons and Callan, 359.
31. Craig E. Johnson. Meeting the Ethical Challenges of Leadership: Casting Light or Shadow. London: SAGE, 2011.
32. Fitzsimmons and Callan, 355.
33. Fitzsimmons and Callan, 356.
34. Fitzsimmons and Callan, 357.

early childhood experiences are a significant contributor to society's perception of male and female leadership ability.[35] So much of this framework remains to be explored, and it will be further discussed in Chapter 2. The Bourdieusian framework may be novel to many but holds prominence in scholarly literature as a valuable source for understanding how social constructs and experiences influence behavior of each gender. It also gives insight into how that influenced behavior enables individuals to navigate the exclusive good old boy network.

Exclusivity of the old boy network erects walls guarding against individuals deemed unworthy of entry. It excludes some men due to lack of social and educational status. Unfortunately, lack of social status and educational opportunities tend to follow individuals and families from one generation to the next, and even more so for women. Education is what we know; whereas, social capital refers to who we know. The saying, "It's not what you know. It's who you know" captures this concept. For hundreds of years, limited education and access to certain social advantages congested our feminine paths with various obstructions. We continue to navigate roadblocks by attaining advanced college degrees and jump hurdles by conforming to unnatural and uncomfortable male-dominated culture only to face the walls of the old boy network.

Exclusivity of the old boy network erects walls guarding against individuals deemed unworthy of entry.

Male Groupthink

Psychology Today states the following:

> Groupthink occurs when a group of well-intentioned people make irrational or non-optimal decisions spurred by the urge to conform or the discouragement of dissent. This problematic or premature consensus may be fueled by a particular agenda or simply because group members value harmony and coherence above rational thinking. In a groupthink situation, group members refrain from expressing doubts and judgments or disagreeing with the consensus. In the interest of making a decision that furthers their group cause, members may ignore any ethical or moral consequences.[36]

---

35. See note 26.
36. Irving L. Janis. "Groupthink." Psychology Today 26, (1971): 43-76.

Again, this has to do with men thinking that women should occupy certain positions and not be included in things that are historically male-dominated. Long-established organizational culture assumes men to be the leaders. Because of this, men believe leadership comes naturally for them. The division of labor at home has a lot to do with this thinking. For the most part, women cook, clean, and raise the children. A majority of men continue to believe that certain roles are gender specific. However, there is a noticeable and drastic shift of this thinking in the millennial mindset. Millennial women are not so easily signing up for domestic duty. More than ever before, men stay at home and equally share in domestic labor.

For this book, male groupthink will focus on how men as a group believe that women should hold certain positions in society or in organizations because of gender. It is so culturally ingrained in their DNA that they will never wholly shake this position. It is just the way men think; it is unspoken but evident. As of right now, male groupthink is the sign of the times for men of certain generations. We should accept it as their truth, leave it alone, and not try to change it because we cannot. As women, however, we can stand in our own truth and not be concerned with male groupthink. Ignoring its existence is the only way to remove it as an obstacle. Ignore its presence, and thereby extinguish its power!

Candidly Speaking

Theories that bind include societal representations limiting our entry to leadership and societal practices hindering our professional advancement. Role Congruity Theory, Social Role Theory, and Glass Cliff Theory are prevalent theories directly related to the challenges to women's leadership advancement in Western culture. These theories create situations in which we have to make choices that have negative results no matter what – situations referred to as double binds. A behavioral double bind is described as "a behavioral norm that creates a situation where a person cannot win no matter what she does."[37] Brescoll's (2016) study describes emotional double binds as the need for women to "walk a line" between expressing enough but not too much

---

37. Oakley, 325.

emotion to avoid the risk of violating stereotypes.[38] Double binds limit women's ability to display a full range of behaviors.[39] Throughout history, double binds have been used to usurp women's power. For example, women are challenged to speak assertively but criticized if they talk too assertively. They are judged for being too feminine and negatively viewed if they are perceived as too masculine. Self-promotion, decisiveness, warmth, and selflessness are all manners of communication expressed freely by men but considered unacceptable behaviors for women. Double binds are socially accepted behaviors that require gender diversity in corporate governance to lessen its effect on organizational cultures. Behavioral double binds are relevant to this book because they represent an aspect of bias against women that is very difficult to pinpoint and therefore hard to set a standard for abatement.

Self-promotion, decisiveness, warmth, and selflessness are all manners of communication expressed freely by men but considered unacceptable behaviors for women.

Theories that bind are the "rock and the hard place" for women, as contemplating exactly how to handle a matter at hand becomes quite a task. Our quandary includes thoughts such as whether or not we should inflect confidence in our voices when we speak up about a situation. Then, we think maybe not because that might give the impression that we are too assertive or even borderline confrontational. Perhaps we should just choose our battles, avoid voicing concerns, and allow certain situations to work themselves out? Taking that route might make us seem indecisive and too passive to fulfill executive leadership roles. Sometimes we simply do not know whether to act in one manner or the other. Therein lies our dilemma and the crux of theories that bind us.

A variety of social constructs contribute to the hindrance of women achieving prominent-level leadership positions. However, one common thread unifies all of those constructs, the Social Role Theory. The Social Role Theory acts as the foundation and greatest influence for the norms, systems, and theories that bind women. This theory basically addresses how society sees gender-focused roles. For instance, men are the providers; women are the nurturers. Men lead; women follow. Men

---

38. Brescoll, 417.
39. Fitzsimmons and Callan.

are aggressive, while women are accommodating and so forth. There has always been the lingering perception that women have certain attributes best suited for nurturing, which has probably been present since the time of the caveman.

Social ideals born from Social Role Theory are a very difficult ideology to break because no matter what happens, women will always bear the children. Admittedly, there are some things innately correct about this theory just because of the way God made us. The Social Role Theory argues the predetermined perception that there are certain roles for men and other roles more suitable for women, even if it relates to the strength required to do a task. One thought often used is that men are naturally stronger by nature, so it only "makes sense" that they are assigned more physically taxing work than we are.

This theory is primarily based on differences between the genders in terms of physical ability and physical attributes. It is so ingrained into our DNA that we walk, talk, and live it. The overt physical, emotional, and psychological makeup of a woman cannot be changed. Furthermore, the whole shero concept is not to try to change what we cannot. The goal is to acknowledge a reality that contributes to hindrances of our leadership achievement and change our behavioral reactions to these hindrances so that they no longer have power over us.

Statistically Speaking

Women in the Workplace, the largest study of the state of women in corporate America, confirms the issue regarding women in leadership. Based on five years of data from almost 600 companies, the 2019 report indicated the following:

- Women are less likely to be hired and promoted to manager. For every 100 men promoted and hired to manager, only 72 women are promoted and hired.
- Men hold 62% of manager-level positions, while women hold just 38%. The number of women decreases at every subsequent level.
- One third of companies set gender representation targets for first-level manager roles, compared to 41% for senior levels of management.

- We can add one million more women to management in corporate America over the next five years if women are hired and promoted to manager at the same rate as men.[40]

These statistics display the blatant disparity of women in leadership roles. It is commonplace and has changed very slowly over time, so it does not represent the pool of talented women. Levels of management represent leadership opportunities. Whether the numbers are analyzed by looking at numerical values or percentages, leadership opportunities for females clearly lag that of our male counterparts. Based on the sheer number of women holding advanced degrees in business with strong line experience, and the drive and leadership skills to run Fortune 500 companies, these numbers reveal how powerful theories, social perceptions, and most of all, how male organizational culture controls and influences women's access to leadership status.

On Another Note

Perhaps the obvious should have been acknowledged from the outset; men and women are different. Physically, socially, emotionally, etc.—men and women operate and interact in distinctly different ways. The in-depth exploration and discussion within this chapter give a candid viewpoint of how those differences are used to frame social perspectives and roles for the genders, which hinders our ascent to leadership. These hindrances continue to create barriers, which rest on society's belief in gendered social roles. Some people in our society still subscribe to the theory that women are born as nurturers, mothers who raise children, and therefore better suited for certain professional roles in society. Even in the 21st century we still struggle with these same biases and prejudices. We still face the constant tug of war for corporate and political positioning with "the good old boys." There are groups that consciously exclude women solely on the basis of gender. Consequently, we try fixing ourselves to fit into the male-dominated culture that currently prevails.

Physically, socially, emotionally, etc.—men and women operate and interact in distinctly different ways.

---

40. McKinsey & Company and LeanIn.org. "Women in the Workplace 2019." (2019). https://womenintheworkplace.com/.

Fitting in a male-dominated culture will not happen easily for us. Conversations preferred among men naturally differ from those of women. Men often engage in conversations that women might consider sexist or degrading. In cases like this, we should accept and find comfort with not being included. However, some of us still play into roles just to fit in. We try to force ourselves to fit into situations so that we can be included. But it is futile. Based on research, female acceptance into heavily-dominated male careers, clubs, professional societies and organizations is virtually nonexistent.[41] Like any dominant subculture, the "old boy network" has a lot to lose if its culture is forced to change and invite female entrants.[42] If large numbers of women ascended to top positions in large corporations, it is quite probable they would challenge the prevailing masculine cultural norms the same way they did when they infiltrated other areas of corporate life.[43] According-ing to research by Oakley, 2000, "Questioning of the need to hide or eliminate emotions in the workplace, the use of sports metaphors, and the importance of golf often associated with the culture of the old boy network would be challenged by an influx of a large number of females into this culture."[44] Trying to change a male-dominated organization that has a fixed mindset into what we want it to be is futile. This is where we as women hit a ceiling with every effort to force our way into a fixed culture.

Over the course of hundreds of years, gender-based prejudices and stereotypes merged to form one-sided norms, systems, and theories that bind us.

Over the course of hundreds of years, gender-based prejudices and stereotypes merged to form one-sided norms, systems, and theories that bind us. One result is the male-dominated culture within leadership. Whether it is fair or not, this is our reality. The goal is not to only present proof that the odds are stacked against our proven efforts, skill sets, or even to wallow in our misfortunes in the realm of leadership. There is so much forward movement happening and more on the brink of taking place that we must continue persevering and preparing for the best. Collectively, we are not only resisting norms, systems, and theories that bind, but we are also forging through. As we forge through, let us embrace who we are naturally and resist the pressure to give up our innate abilities.

41. Brescoll; Eagly and Karau; Fitzsimmons and Callan; Oakley; and Schein.
42. Oakley, 329.
43. See note 42.
44. Oakley, 325.

A Foundational Understanding

In this chapter we addressed the foundational problems that create ties that bind women to societal opinions and social constructs that create barriers to entry into the upper echelons of leadership. This foundation of understanding is critical for the journey of enlightenment that we are about to take together. As we evolve into our natural place in society as sheroes, understanding the headwinds we will face will help us to change the trajectory to one more conducive to our success. This foundational information is essential for current and aspiring women leaders as it clarifies the obstacles and their origination. Equipped with this knowledge, we can stop trying to navigate these obstacles. Instead we can begin ignoring the "noise" seeking to distract us, cutting our own paths, and creating our own opportunities.

In the words of the "Women in the Workplace" study, "The broken rung is the biggest obstacle women face."[45] We may not be able to change the societal perception of women, but we can change our approach to creating opportunities for each other by building our own ladders one rung at a time. The first rung of that ladder includes an honest self and collective reflection of what we might be doing to exacerbate or fall prey to the theories that bind.

Moving Forward

We acknowledge theories that bind for the reality they are but continue to move forward towards cultivating and building upon our great potential. Thus, the discussion in the next chapter is imperative. In the next chapter we examine how women may contribute to gender bias and negative perceptions of our leadership ability. We will take a closer look at current and past situations that reveal how we unconsciously fall into stereotypical traps.

---

45. McKinsey & Company and LeanIn.org.

MELANIE BRAGG
LAWYER – AUTHOR- MENTOR

I am just honored and blessed and unbelievably ecstatic that that I did go to law school and that I have been a lawyer for 38 years. And, I only had one job which was at the Court of Appeals as a briefing attorney my first year out of law school and I got to know all the judges. And I have had my own practice, I never worked for a firm, I never had the neutral male backdrop, and I don't know why but I always do jazz hands with that [talking about the male backdrop], but you know a lot of times, especially for a young woman, it's like they don't trust you unless they know a man is really behind you, to make a decision. So with me, not having a man back there really making the decisions, there was a big sort of push back, and you could almost SEE it in their body language. So I didn't really see myself as a pioneer or trendsetter back then, I was just doing what came naturally to me. To eat what you kill. It never dawned on me that I was doing something revolutionary. But it's really neat to stand here 38 years later. You know, there have been all kinds of dips and hollows, ups and downs in the course of things but I'm standing here now telling you that I am so happy to be a part of what I consider the world's greatest profession. I love it, it's awesome.

In terms of professional associations and organizations, I say, about leadership, some people have it naturally, but it can be learned. I just was lucky enough to have it naturally. When I was in law school, I joined the law student division board of directors, there was no opposition, I don't think anybody even knew what it was. I decided to have a little placement program at the Annual Bar convention that year, and I asked the president of the state bar in Texas (The King!) to come and speak to the law students. And everybody looked at me like I was crazy for asking, but he came, and he is still a very good friend of mine all these years later. I think I learned that lesson early on: Start at the top and work your way down. I didn't have anybody tell me to do that, I just did it naturally but it worked well for me, so well that they kept doing it year after year and eventually it turned into what is now called "The Texas Job Fair" and for about 25 years, all the placement directors of law schools knew that its genesis was my program. I mean, I never got credit for it, but if you are a true leader, you don't need credit, you just have the honor of getting to start things so I've always been able to be a little bit of a spark plug or energy booster for the ideas that I get naturally and carry them forward.

Chapter II

The Trap

I am impassioned by the dilemma I see women in today that traps them into societal norms and hinders their progress toward equality. Because of the subconscious effects of entrapment, potential lies dormant in many women. Somewhere along the way in my personal evolution, I realized that all humans have the exact same capabilities. I also came to realize that undernourished capabilities seem nonexistent. These seemingly absent capabilities that fall into the trap of societal expectations will not thrive. A planted seed will not grow without water and sunlight, but when the sun is allowed to shine on that planted seed, and the rain waters that seed, chances of its germination and growth are highly probable. As sheroes, our sun and water come from within. We are all capable of growing and thriving. Let us not allow societal traps to steal our glory!

I honestly do not remember where or when, but somewhere along my journey, I began to feel blessed. That feeling pushed me to challenge myself beyond what society expected of me. Sure, I stumbled and made plenty of mistakes, but I allowed none of that to stop my forward motion. I realized early that my weapon against frail expectations was my ability to think and reason. I earned my bachelors, masters, and most recently my doctorate degree. During all of this, life happened. I married, had two children, divorced, and completely uprooted my life to move from California to Texas. I say all of this to provide hope for a society of women who at some point missed the mark because they drank the "kool aid" handed to them by major malevolent influences in present day society. The abnormality of these influences is made evident when the "sun" of truth is shined on them. Enabling the light of truth to shine brightly through the darkness of entrapment is my goal in this chapter.

A Moment of Reflection

Placing the blame for our plight in leadership spares us some of the responsibility. We are not responsible for the establishment of social constructs or the barriers they cause. We cannot control those things. However, we are not completely helpless. What remains in our sphere of control is our response. Some may ask, "How can we respond to make progressive steps towards our leadership goals?" The short answer is to reflect and evaluate. Once we evaluate the psychological effects of those restrictive social norms, systems, and ties that bind us and note our responses for the purpose of altering our outcome, we will be on the path to making progress despite social conditioning and societal limitations.

Pavlov's dog experiments played a critical role in the discovery of one of the most important concepts in psychology, classical conditioning.[46] Classical conditioning emphasizes the importance of learning from the environment and supports nurture over nature. When society creates an unhealthy norm, the response is often unhealthy. Women have been conditioned to respond a certain way to societal norms for their advancement. In this chapter, "The Trap," I invite you into the discussion about how we almost inherently trap ourselves into the very societal perceptions that bind us by our own thought processes. Bourdieusian framework will be further explained in this chapter, as it supports this discussion. We will also discuss double binds which supports the concept that "you are damned if you do and damned if you don't."

46. Ivan P. Pavlov. The Work of the Digestive Glands. London: Griffin, 1897/1902.

Entrapment

As we continue to become enlightened about the invisible forces that women continue to fight against, the shero story continues to unfold. Moreover, the theories we just discussed have trackable consequences for women. As the journey of the shero continues to unfold, so do the situations that we find ourselves in.

The Cambridge dictionary defines trap as "a device or hole for catching animals or people and preventing their escape" or "a dangerous or unpleasant situation which you have got into and from which it is difficult or impossible to escape."[47] Both definitions are horrible predicaments to be in, and it is unfortunate that we as women often find ourselves in the middle of psychological traps. We seem to constantly compete in attempts to overcome inequities and

As we continue to become enlightened about the invisible forces that women continue to fight against, the shero story continues to unfold.

prove that we are not the stereotypes haunting us—particularly the theories and prejudices that society projects when it comes to women and leadership. We often find ourselves constantly fighting to prove that we are not falsehoods projected by certain societal constructs. Our constant fight to prove ourselves makes us slaves to the very inequities that we are trying to overcome. However, this bewildering entrapment can be avoided.

Point of Inquisition

As women, we tend to compete directly with men to prove that we are just as good as they are when competition is not the answer. A lot of energy is put into trying to prove that we are not the weak and emotional wrecks incapable of leadership. Trying to prove something negatively ingrained in the minds of the masses takes a lot of energy and focus.

Gender-biased traps are hard not to fall into if we are constantly trying to avoid them. Trying to prove that our skills are just as good, if not better than men's is a job in itself. Men's innate DNA and skill set prepares them to excel in situations that society deems more suitable for the mas-

47. "Trap." Cambridge Dictionary. https://dictionary.cambridge.org/us/dictionary/english/trap.

culine species. Therefore, it is a fixed fight when women decide to combat that stereotype. It is a fight that will not be won in the sense that we cannot; women literally cannot compete with men in certain areas because of physiological and psychological makeup. Our structure is different—muscle groups, the very enzymes that go through our bodies are all different.

One major revelation that came out in my research combats the theory that women are too emotional. Through research, I found that both men and women are equally emotional.[48] However, the difference lies in the way that they express their emotions. Women might express their emotions externally by crying or getting upset; whereas, men in the same situation may get angry. Both of these responses are emotional. We are different, and different enzymes go through our bodies creating different responses in a male versus a female. Testosterone fuels males' responses while progesterone influences ours. As women, we should embrace our differences and use those differences as a power of our own in our own right.

Many women have entered contact sports like boxing and football, which in the long run, can really damage their bodies, especially reproductively. Let me bring some clarity here. I am not saying that we should not participate in contact sports. We have the freedom to do whatever we want. That is one of the privileges of living in a free democracy. We are free to do those things, but the reasoning behind doing them is often flawed by our need to compete on a man's level. When women do those things for the wrong reasons, we reinforce the very traps that bind us. Whether consciously or unconsciously, some of us tend to play into the traps themselves by continually trying to fit in, especially in male-dominated situations. Our efforts to fit in distract us from sharpening our natural skills and using them for a greater good.

Statistically Speaking

Earlier, I mentioned the differences between the physical make-up of males and females. I will now discuss a few definitive ways that men and women are distinctly different. To preface this discussion, I cite Natalie Wolchover's

48. Brescoll, 417.

concise definition and explanation of the term regarding differences between men and women makeup. She states the following:

> *"Sexual dimorphism" is the scientific term for physical differences between males and females of a species. Men and women are more physically similar than different. Nonetheless, a few key distinctions in physiques set men and women apart. Some of them are designed to suit each sex for the role it plays in reproduction, while others exist to help us tell each other apart and aid in our mutual attraction.*[49]

Here are some of the cited differences:

- Women have breasts; whereas, men have flat chests (but still with nipples on them).
- Men and women both have cartilage surrounding their voice boxes, but because men have bigger boxes (which give them deeper voices), their chunks of cartilage protrude more. This gives them neck lumps called Adam's apples.
- The more testosterone a man has, the stronger his brow, cheekbones, and jawline. Meanwhile, the more estrogen a woman has, the wider her face, fuller her lips, and the higher her eyebrows. In short, sex hormones control the divergence of male and female facial features.
- In general, men are more muscular than women. Women are just over half as strong as men in their upper bodies, and about two-thirds as strong in their lower bodies.
- While the male metabolism burns calories faster, the female metabolism tends to convert more food to fat. Women store the extra fat in their breasts, hips, buttocks, and as subcutaneous fat in the bottom layer of their skin, which gives women's skin its softer, plumper feel.
- Male and female bodies are well-designed for each gender's role in a primitive society. Women are built for carrying and birthing children, so they must have wider hips and keep extra fat in store for the ordeal of pregnancy. Men, free from the requirements of childbirth, benefit from being as strong and lithe as possible, both in their search for food, and when in competition with other men.

---

49. Natalie Wolchover. "Men vs. Women: Our Key Physical Differences Explained." LiveScience, September 22, 2011. https://www.livescience.com/33513-men-vs-women-our-physical-differences-explained.html.

Unlike males, our physiological purpose as females in the species is to replicate. Our physiological makeup supports that premise. However, we are all unique individuals with the free will to do anything we desire to do. My point is that we can get caught up in the competition to become what we are not to prove a point, when our innate skills and talents lie elsewhere. Each of us should be alert and aware of what that looks like, instead of morphing ourselves into what society says we should be. Let us stand in our own individual truths.

Just as distinct differences exist between men and women, they also occur between women. Take my sister and me for example. I am the type of person that I am. I am aggressive. When I see something I want, I go after it wholeheartedly. I am really trying to compete with myself – to force myself to constantly do better and look internally for the things that I could do better based upon what I go after. On the other hand, my sister is a born nurturer. She loves children. She has raised and taken care of children much of her entire life. She had seven children, and each one of her children have had quite a few of their own. Thus, her entire life has revolved around being that maternal person whom she has perfected. My sister and I accept ourselves for who we innately are. We work within and hone our gifted abilities to make the best life possible for ourselves and our families. As a collective group, women should do the same.

Unlike males, our physiological purpose as females in the species is to replicate.

The Bourdieusian Framework

Pierre Bourdieu was a French sociologist, anthropologist, philosopher, and renowned intellectual. His primary work related to the dynamics of power in society, especially the diverse and subtle ways power is transferred and social order is maintained within and across generations. His frameworks studied the differential treatment of girls and boys in traditional Western society which promotes gender-biased attitudes in leadership and raising girls. In essence, this framework speaks of the intergenerational disparities in a social setting, specifically the acquisition of two very important embodiments of cultural capital. It speaks to how we gain capital as we grow to become who or what we are trying to be, especially in leadership positions.

There are two distinct concepts I would like to address. There is the cultural capital which includes deeply-ingrained habits, skills, and dispositions that we possess due to our life experiences. Bourdieu refers to this cultural capital as habitus, which is the way society becomes the positive in a people's experiences to form lasting dispositions. Basically, cultural capital embeds trained capacities and structured propensities to the way we think, feel, and act. The premise is that our habits are ingrained in us from birth and even in the womb before birth.[50]

The Bourdieusian Framework also points out the concept of capital, which extends beyond the notion of material assets to social capital. Cultural capital is a means by which each of us creates and transforms our central roles in society. Our ability to accumulate capital determines the power that we obtain culturally in a society. Men are automatically expected to possess that power. This notion is ingrained and deposited into them at an early age. They are raised in a way that they acquire more social capital in terms of leadership from birth.

Studies show that the accumulation of this capital starts at birth and is nurtured throughout the social habitus used to raise boys versus girls.[51] It is critical to understand that we still live under the social habitus common to Western culture, which began at birth and existed throughout our entire lives.

Double Binds

As discussed in Chapter 1, theories that bind are societal norms that have evolved over many centuries. As women push for and incite change, these theories continue to have profound effects on women's maneuvering within society. As a cause and effect example, binding theories, the cause has the effect of creating challenging predicaments. One such predicament is known as a double bind.

Double binds affect how women lead. Oakley (2000) defines a double bind as "a behavioral norm that creates a situation where a person cannot win no matter what she does."[52] Research shows that double binds severely limit women's abilities to engage in a full range of influencing behaviors by challenging their leadership style as either too masculine or too feminine.[53] Double binds have been used throughout history by those with

---

50. Fitzsimmons and Callan, 357.
51. Doey, Coplan, and Kingsbury; Fitzsimmons and Callan.
52. Oakley, 325.
53. Oakley, 326.

the power to oppress those without power. Most often, the victims (those without power) are women. This creates a potential trap for women. Double binds create a unique challenge because they are often not articulated but present themselves as obstacles to surmount. Oakley's research points to self-consciousness that women in power experience when challenged by double binds, which can drain energy away from important tasks if women take double binds too seriously. Double binds continue to pose a direct challenge to female authority and represent a very common trap that we fall into as we try to balance their effects.

Double binds are very interesting traps. Essentially, they are situations where "you're damned if you do and damned if you don't. Women are often caught between two irreconcilable demands. Either choice is going to be viewed as negative. A probable example of this is the 2020 presidential election. When Joe Biden, the current presumptive democratic nominee, announced that he will name a female running mate, the media briefly focused on allegations of past inappropriate behavior by Joe Biden. He was accused of inappropriate behavior with female colleagues. Out of several claims, one woman who worked with Biden in 1992 brought allegations against him for touching her inappropriately and penetrating her. He denies the allegations.

Double binds are very interesting traps. Essentially, they are situations where "you're damned if you do and damned if you don't.

This brings the male groupthink back to the forefront where inappropriate behavior towards women in the past was swept under the rug—similar to the sexual misconduct allegations against President Donald Trump. The power behind male groupthink lies in its members' overwhelming desire for cohesiveness. The Republican Party repeatedly affirms this power as they appear to value unity over making the best or ethical decision. They seem to value unity so highly that they risk falling prey to lost individualism by foregoing individual beliefs and principles in favor of the group. It no longer matters what the individual believes or wants; it is a matter of yielding to group influence. The prevailing groupthink situation in this current administration demonstrates the desire for cohesion, includes the derogation of dissenters, and implements the placement and influence of mindguards.[54] Mindguards intercept attempts to limit or question group

---

54. "Mindguard." Word Finder. https://findwords.info/term/mindguard.

decisions. Mindguards are individuals who ensure that dissent is kept to a minimum thereby preserving male groupthink position. Male groupthink is so powerful within the Republican party that no matter what the president says or does, the majority of them will stick by him because of their loyalty to not upset the group's accepted norm. More than likely, similar accepted norms concealed previous allegations made against Biden.

Let us ponder Biden's presidential scenario again. Given past allegations of misconduct and his decision to choose a female running mate one may ask, "Is this a clever strategy as a way to dismiss misconduct or true desire to name the most competent, suitable running mate on the merits of her ability, strengths and experience? The question is based on all that happened with Biden's past allegations as well as his choice of a female running mate. This is indeed a scenario worth deeper analysis.

A recent article in The Cut Magazine talks about a woman putting herself in this very position. Whoever decides to run with Biden is basically voicing support for his campaign.[55] Now, the question becomes, "how is this woman going to be viewed?" Is she going to look like a hypocrite for agreeing to be on a ticket with a man who was accused of this type of behavior? Maybe at some point she voiced her opinions against women being assaulted, and now she is going to be his running mate, the running mate of a man accused of assault against a woman? Hence, a possible double bind is created simply because Joe Biden chose a female running mate.

Congresswoman Alexandria Ocasio-Cortez recently gave her support to Joe Biden, but she is also a progressive woman who fights against sexual harassment and assault. Now that she is promoting and endorsing Biden, she has to retract things she said about his past behaviors or act as if she did not mention them. This is a prime example of a double-bind type of situation. She definitely would have been criticized (damned) if she did not initially speak out against the harassment and assault of women. Now that she supports a presidential candidate accused of sexual assault, she gets criticized (damned) for seemingly supporting perpetrators of the very thing she spoke out against. Once she expressed support for Joe Biden, people began tweeting against her and calling her a hypocrite. This particular situation warrants a reflection. Is this the only situation where a woman who

---

55. Rebecca Traister. "The Biden Trap." The Cut. The Cut, April 28, 2020. https://www.thecut.com/2020/04/the-biden-trap-woman-vice-president.html.

distinguished herself as a feminist or an advocate against attacks on women changed? Is that a call for hypocrisy? Double binds present extremely challenging positions, which may not change any time soon because we are still building and growing stronger when it comes to advantageously positioning ourselves to avoid falling into traps of inequities against women.

The woman that Biden named as his running mate will find herself facing a very interesting double bind for sure, particularly if she publicly advocates or has advocated against sexual harassment against women. It will be interesting to see how she answers questions regarding her stance on the subject as the running mate of a man accused of the very thing people would expect her to advocate against. The female vice-presidential candidate will likely reach a precarious situation—one facing questions or criticisms that are going to come her way, especially if she has fought against sexual harassment. She, like many of us, will find herself fighting against the trap of the double bind.

Avoiding the Trap

Our aim is to avoid "The Trap." In order to accomplish that, each of us should reflect then do a personal reality check. When reflecting, have an honest conversation with yourself by periodically asking, "What am I trying to accomplish?" The answer will evolve as time goes on. What you set out to accomplish during your twenties will undoubtedly evolve into something different in your fifties. If you are like most of

Our aim is to avoid "The Trap." us, you externalize your intentions based upon what you see and experience in the world and society. This is true because our external environment is our first teacher. Societal norms influence how we determine what appropriate behavior is. No matter what, work towards your desired goal at that time. This is where the personal reality check comes into play. If you want to speak out against brutality and sexual assault against women, do so unapologetically. If you want to be a boxer or a wrestler, then be that, and make that your truth. Do not let it become something that you try to prove just because society says you cannot do it.

It might seem as though I am pointing the finger at you because—well, I am. However, I do so with the audacity to encourage your individual reflection and growth. In order for women as a group to avoid "The Trap," it will require us to do more than acknowledge or address societal constraints. Each of us must individually work our potential to its fullest. That includes you and me.

Now is the time to revolutionize our thinking and stop contributing to obsolete social theories regarding gender and leadership. We possess everything we need to establish a new paradigm for women in leadership roles. The key to avoiding the traps that hinder our forward motion is to realize that we control the narrative and are ultimately in charge of their demise. If we continue allowing dysfunctional societal norms about gender in our society to hold us captive or guide our choices, then the shortcomings of traditional thinking regarding the role of women will continue to adversely affect our destiny. Now that we are aware, we can more effectively change the plot of an age-old narrative. We can also raise our daughters to think differently by owning who they are at an early age and dispel the myths of theories regarding women and leadership in the 21st century. Right here is an excellent place for the Nike slogan, "Just Do It!" We must. We can. And we will.

Moving Forward

In the next chapter, I will discuss the slippery slope of the Glass Cliff Theory. I will also provide some modern examples, which include a review of the challenges former President Barack Obama and 2016 presidential candidate Hillary Clinton encountered.

KIKI KOYMARIANOS
ENTREPRENEUR - REAL ESTATE CONSULTANT – SPEAKER – COACH – TRAINER – MOM - CREDIT EXPERT

I got introduced to Women On A Mission To Earn Commission (WOAM-TEC) when I lived in Boca Raton in South Florida. I went to one chapter that was just forming and I was like "Oh, this is nice," and then we moved to Texas. I didn't know anybody. I went to all these networking events and thought, "None of these really give me the feeling I had in WOAMTEC back in Florida." So, I called the former owner of WOAMTEC and said "I want to start a chapter in Texas," I was brand new to the area, I didn't know anybody, I was trying to figure out what the area was like, I was trying to figure out my own business. When you are a realtor, you need to meet people – other-wise how are you going to build your business? Kathleen was the owner and she said, "You really don't fit our requirements, you don't have a big enough database… but I am going to do it, because I have to get something started." Long story short, I was truly a woman on a mission to build that chapter!

My son was 4 years old at the time, he would stay at the daycare, he was probably the last one picked up, but I was going out, networking. I was going to vendor events, wherever there were people, I was there, collecting business cards. I built a database of about 2,500 people. Where there is a will, there is a way. So I built the biggest chapter, we have about 120 members and out of that we started about 8 more chapters in the area and we went all the way down to Sugarland. And in 2012 an opportunity arose, and I bought the organization, so I own it now, nationwide. My main thing is, I believe I have without a doubt met, the most inspiring, most driven women, most amazing women though this organization. We are in Florida, California, Texas. It's amazing what women can do when they put their heads together and build true sisterhood.

It's important to empower women first because we are the role models of our households. Our kids look up to us, so if the kids see their moms working well with other women, they see their moms being successful, being happy, being empowered, that gives them another aspect of life to investigate.

I truly believe that women are the pillars of our society and I think we all need to stick together and do our best to empower, educate and elevate each other.

Chapter III

The Glass Cliff Theory

Being an African-American female in the financial services industry, I have found myself, throughout my career, in positions where I was not expected to succeed. One particular situation that I remember vividly was during one of the many financial advisor summits in Scottsdale, Arizona. As one of the few women in the group and the only African-American woman at the time, I was not expected to survive for the next event. White men dominate the financial services industry. It is a difficult field for women to succeed in because investors, especially from the baby boomer generation, mostly trust white men to handle their money. At the summit, I overheard a group of men taking bets that I would not be around for the next summit and paying each other off for lost bets that I would make it to the current one. They laughed and said, "She is doomed. No one with any real money will work with her." The wonderful white man who appointed me to the organization wanted me to succeed, but, quite frankly, did not think that I would. That was in 2005. Today in 2020, I am one of the few top female African-American advisors in the country. I accepted the challenge of being silently doubted but used it as my fuel to excel. I did not let the banter of men alter my course.

Although I persevered, I was not oblivious to others' lack of confidence in my professional and leadership abilities. I knew doubt circulated in the air, but I did not understand the underlying theory fueling that doubt. I am not sure if a specific term had been coined at that time. Through my studies, I began to understand how the Glass Cliff Theory correlates with events that happened in my professional and leadership career and that same journey of other women.

A Moment of Reflection

That thing, the seemingly impenetrable barrier, keeps some of us women from moving to the next level. Many times, we look up with optimism, and it seems like all we can see is opportunity before us. Not so—it is only a mirage of opportunity. Since the blood, sweat, tears, and after hours of work proved futile, we know for a fact that something is there holding us back. We might not be able to see it, but we know it is there. What is there is called a glass ceiling. The glass ceiling warrants attention as we connect it with the glass cliff and how the two are set to operate in unison, one after the other. Women who successfully penetrate the glass ceiling are met with another challenge; they must work to get a firm grip that will help them avoid sliding off of the glass cliff.

Merriam Webster defines glass ceiling as "an intangible barrier within a hierarchy that prevents women or minorities from obtaining upper-level positions."[56] The term glass ceiling and its meaning are well known and understood. However, its relationship to the Glass Cliff Theory is rarely realized or explored. You followed along in Chapter 1 where I defined and briefly discussed the Glass Cliff Theory. Once again, I welcome you into Chapter 2's discussion in which I expound upon that definition and give examples of the theory by mentioning some of the female leaders it has affected in top organizations. Afterwards, our discussion will follow the phenomenon to another level by considering its relationship to and association with minorities of the 2008 presidential election. We will think through its connection to politics of the presidential election and discuss how the glass cliff affected presidential candidate Hillary Clinton. Clinton was able to penetrate the glass ceiling and rose to be the first female candidate making it to be the democratic nominee only to fall off of the glass cliff. We will discuss Clinton's plight later in the chapter. I will also discuss the perceived relationship between the glass cliff phenomenon and the election of this country's first African-American president, President Barack Hussein Obama.

The Glass Cliff Theory is a theoretical phenomenont that sheds light on how the modern woman ascertains her fragile leadership power in a male-dominated society.

---

56. "Glass Ceiling." Merriam Webster Dictionary. https://www.merriam-webster.com/dictionary/glass%20ceiling.

Cornerstone of the Glass Cliff

The Glass Cliff Theory is a theoretical phenomenon that sheds light on how the modern woman ascertains her fragile leadership power in a male-dominated society. In this chapter, I share multiple examples of how the theory has been studied and evaluated with the hope that you will see the synchronicity of its intent and be better positioned to strategize its demise. Grace Back had this to say about the Glass Cliff Theory:

> It's a new theory that suggests women are much more likely to be ap-pointed to top jobs – like CEO or Prime Minister – when the company or country in question is in serious trouble.
>
> Researchers Dr. Michelle Ryan and Professor Alex Haslam coined the term 'glass cliff' after investigating women in positions of power; namely how they got to the top and how long they stayed there.[57]

Forbes Magazine Senior Contributor, Kathy Caprino stated the following in her article:

> The glass cliff concept was developed by Dr. Michelle Ryan and Professor Alex Haslam from the School of Psychology at the University of Exeter. As described in Ryan and Haslam's research, the glass cliff examines what hap-pens when women (and other minority groups) take on leadership roles. Ex-tending the metaphor of the glass ceiling, 'the glass cliff' research has found that women tend to be appointed to leadership positions under very differ-ent circumstances than men. More specifically, this research suggests that women are more likely to be appointed to leadership positions that are as-sociated with an increased risk of criticism and failure. Women's leadership positions can thus be seen as more precarious than those of men.[58]

Yael Oelbaum provides an academic perspective on the theory. She present-ed the following evidence about the Glass Cliff Theory:

> The glass cliff effect describes a real-world phenomenon in which women are more likely to be appointed to precarious leadership positions in poorly performing organizations, while men are more likely to be ap-pointed to stable leadership positions in successful organizations (Ryan

57. Grace Back. "Is the 'Glass Cliff Theory' Happening to the Today Show's New All-Female Panel?" Marie Claire, January 10, 2019. https://www.marieclaire.com.au/glass-cliff-thoery.
58. Kathy Caprino. "The 'Glass Cliff' Phenomenon That Senior Female Leaders Face Today and How to Avoid It." Forbes. Forbes Magazine, October 20, 2015. https://www.forbes.com/sites/kathycaprino/2015/10/20/the-glass-cliff-phenomenon-that-senior-female-leaders-face-today-and-how-to-avoid-it/.

& Haslam, 2005). This effect represents a subtle, yet dangerous, form of gender discrimination that may limit workplace diversity as well as women's ability to become successful leaders. Importantly, research exploring why women are preferred for more perilous leadership positions is lacking. The main focus of this dissertation is to systematically organize previous theory and empirically examine processes underlying the glass cliff effect ... Findings from both studies most strongly demonstrate that females are likely to be preferred over males when being promoted to a precarious position as a way for the organization to signal change. Theoretical implications of the study findings regarding gender and leadership as well as practical implications regarding organizational procedures and women's careers are discussed.[59]

Susanna Whawell, PhD Researcher at University of Manchester, presents another academic perspective about the Glass Cliff Theory:

The glass ceiling is an idea familiar to many. It refers to the invisible barrier that seems to exist in many fields and which prevents women from achieving senior positions. Less well-known, but arguably a more pernicious problem, is the "glass cliff". Originally recognized by academics Michelle Ryan and Alex Haslam back in 2005, this is the phenomenon of women making it to the boardroom but finding themselves disproportionately represented in untenable leadership positions.

Ryan and Haslam presented evidence that women were indeed starting to secure seats at boardroom tables. But the problem was that their positions were inherently unstable. These women would then find themselves in an unsustainable leadership position from which they would be ousted with evidence of apparent failure. The title of their paper sums it up: "women are over-represented in precarious leadership positions".

Subsequent research in an array of environments has demonstrated that this is not an isolated issue, nor is it unique to certain industries or geographical locations. It reveals that women in top leadership positions seem to be routinely handed inherently unsolvable problems.[60]

These are problems that they strive very hard to address – but no matter the effort, these problems cannot be solved. The women in charge are then still held personally accountable for failure, ultimately leading to their resignation or dismissal. This creates a damaging, self-fulfilling prophecy

59. Yael S. Oelbaum. "Understanding the Glass Cliff Effect: Why Are Female Leaders Being Pushed Toward the Edge?" (2016): 82. CUNY Academic Works. https://academicworks.cuny.edu/gc_etds/1597.
60. Susanna Whawell. "Women Are Shattering the Glass Ceiling Only to Fall off the Glass Cliff." The Conversation, February 18, 2020. https://theconversation.com/women-are-shattering-the-glass-ceiling-only-to-fall-off-the-glass-cliff-94071.

that women are unsuitable for leadership positions. Not only does it knock the confidence of the woman in question, it also makes organizations wary of recruiting women to these positions.

These are only a few noted perspectives regarding the existence of the glass cliff phenomenon. However, a common thread between each is the failure of women in senior-ranking positions. This is the heart of the Glass Cliff Theory, and it is accompanied by a variety of attitudes that construct previously discussed norms and systems.

The Glass Cliff Theory aids in the examination of the interaction between societal perceptions and organizational factors which undermine women's successful attainment and tenure in the upper echelons of management and leadership positions across the board. The theory is the way by which those in control (usually men) allow a minority or woman to ascend to a viewership position where the risk of failure is extremely high. The theory adds to the dimension of male majority rule which delves into how men control women's upward mobility.

Point of Inquisition

The problem with glass cliff appointments relates to the presumption of expendability. In essence, women are put in high risk positions to be used as scapegoats and shoulder the blame if things go terribly wrong. Glass cliff appointments are one of many barriers to upward mobility and sustainability for women in leadership positions and can be affirmed from multiple well-documented resources. Nonetheless, unethical recruitment practices that increase the chances for women to advance to glass cliff appointments require continued research. The advancement of women to leadership positions shows significant strides over the last century. There are more female CEO's, judges, senators, business owners, and world leaders than ever before in the history of the world. Despite optimistic growth in female representation, leadership positions continue to be male dominated. A scan across Fortune 500 companies and government positions reflect that women remain underrepresented. A respondent from Ryan, Hasalm, and Postmes' study testing the glass cliff phenomenon had this to say:

I think the glass cliff is another form of the glass ceiling, intended to block women's passage up the ranks. Women will be put in glass cliff positions because there is a resentment of ambitious women who are often seen as threatening or difficult (not just by men) and also because it gives those who appoint them the excuse that they do allow women (superficially) equal opportunities and therefore allows them to avoid any charge of sexism.[61]

Essentially, the glass cliff is a façade. Its deception gives false hope to aspiring female leaders. Some women exert great energy to climb the leadership ladder. They wait with a desperate patience just for the chance to flex their skill sets and demonstrate quality leadership. However, leadership chances rooted in glass cliff appointments do not count as opportunities anticipated by those waiting with immeasurable potential. Glass cliff opportunities truthfully set out to misuse and toss aside women's time and talents but preserve a male-dominated culture of leadership. It is almost as if the value women work so hard to build and strengthen is deliberately set as a sacrifice.

Statistically Speaking

In an effort to explain obstacles that executive-level leaders face and ways they can avoid them, Kathy Caprino stated:

The most compelling piece of data that surprised me was that women are more likely to be promoted to the top – whether it's CEO or at any C-suite level – when the company is facing a downturn or a crisis. That's when boards are more open to appointing someone other than the traditional white, male CEO. And among CEOs leaving office over the past 10 years, a higher share of women has been forced out than men (38% of women vs. 27% of men), because when a company isn't recovering from a crisis, it's often the people at the top who get axed. Look at some of the female CEOs today, and it's easy to spot the so-called "glass cliff" hires. Marissa Mayer at Yahoo, Meg Whitman at Hewlett Packard, Mary Barra at General Motors, Irene Rosenfeld at Mondelez (formerly Kraft) – all these women were appointed to the top job in order to turn their respective

---

61. Michelle K. Ryan, S. Alexander Haslam, and Tom Postmes. "Reactions to the Glass Cliff: Gender Differences in Explanations for the Precariousness of Women's Leadership Positions." Journal of Organizational Change Management 20, no. 2 (2007): 182–97. https://doi.org/10.1108/09534810710724748.

companies around. To date, all of these women have kept their lucrative jobs, but other female CEOs haven't been so lucky. For example, former Yahoo CEO Carol Bartz; former head of Merrill Lynch Smith Barney, Sallie Krawcheck; former co-President of Morgan Stanley, Zoe Cruz, and former Avon CEO, Andrea Jung – these are just some of the women who essentially fell off the glass cliff."[62]

Taking a closer look at a few of the female CEO's mentioned in Caprino's statement illustrates the circumstances upon which they were appointed. Denise Morrison of Campbell Soup, Phebe Novakovic with General Dynamics, Meg Whitman at Hewlett Packard, Mary Barra at General Motors, and Irene Rosenfeld at Mondelez (formerly Kraft) – all of these women were appointed to the most visible position in their organizations during sex scandals, huge operating losses, accounting scandals, and major reconstruction. As forward thinkers, each of them likely had researched and analyzed the entire situation before taking it on, so they knew what they were getting into. These women accepted risky appointments expecting to turn their respective companies around at precarious times. While glass cliff assignments are risky, and failure may derail careers, these women fearlessly accepted the challenge.

While glass cliff assignments are risky, and failure may derail careers, these women fearlessly accepted the challenge.

To date, all of these women continue to hold these prestigious positions, but others (such as individuals Caprino mentions) have not been so lucky. They were either dismissed or resigned. As Kathy Caprino puts it, these women essentially "fell off the glass cliff." As of June 1, 2020, there are 33 female CEO's of Fortune 500 companies.

Looking at numbers only gives us a piece of the picture. Numbers do not lie. They are hard facts. They paint a clear picture of the underrepresentation of women in executive leadership roles. However, they are incapable of showing us soft data, such as what outstanding women leaders say, how they handle themselves in challenging situations, and exactly what makes them worthy of executive leadership appointments.

Perhaps, we should take a closer look at Phebe Nokovich who was appointed as CEO of General Dynamics in 2013 at a time when the company was suffering a $2 billion loss in the previous quarter. Nokovich continues to lead General Dynamics, and the company is better off

---

62. See note 57.

as a result. During a *Washington* Post interview, she was asked, "Did you think a woman could become the CEO of a defense company?" She answered:

> *So, I have always worked in the national security environment, which was heavily male. I never really thought about the difference between men and women in the workplace, although we are different. So, I didn't really think about the maleness of the organization. What attracted me to General Dynamics is that it was different. I'm not an engineer. I have not risen through the ranks from 25-years old. I've had a fairly ... unusual background. And the CEO and chairman at the time was a trial attorney from Chicago. And I thought, oh, there's a bit of an iconoclastic culture here. And maybe there's a place for me. You know, so much in life is about finding your place, whether it's with your family, in your community, your nation, and in your company. And there was a place for me.*[63]

Phebe Nokovich epitomizes the fearlessness and fortitude necessary to not only stand as a female leader during a difficult time but to also lead with valor and competence.

Another example is Meg Whitman. She was appointed to the CEO position at Hewlett Packard during the time of slow growth. The previous CEO, a male, stepped down. I imagine that there was a lot of tension in the company when she was put in charge. Announcement of her appointment to the position included a short speech by her predecessor, Ray Lane. During the announcement, Lane stated:

> *We are fortunate to have someone of Meg Whitman's caliber and experience step up to lead. We are at a critical moment and we need renewed leadership to successfully implement our strategy and take advantage of the market opportunities ahead. Meg is a technology visionary with a proven track record of execution. She is a strong communicator who is customer focused with deep leadership capabilities.*[64]

These women, like so many other capable, competent, and fearless leaders, consciously make the choice to accept risky appointments, and contrary to the Glass Cliff Theory, they thrive!

63. Aaron Gregg. "General Dynamics CEO Phebe Novakovic Recounts Her National Security Journey, Takes a Jab at Silicon Valley." The Washington Post. The Washington Post Company, June 28, 2019. https://www.washington-post.com/business/2019/06/28/general-dynamics-ceo-phebe-novakovic-recounts-her-national-security-journey-takes-jab-silicon-valley/.
64. Hewlett Packard. "HP Names Meg Whitman President and Chief Executive Officer." News Release, September 22, 2011. https://www.sec.gov/Archives/edgar/data/47217/000110465911052939/a11-26875_1ex99d1.htm.

On the other hand, some women are deprived of opportunities to lead because of their perceived competence and the imminent success. This was the case during the 2016 presidential election during which formidable candidate, Hillary Clinton, experienced an unexplainable loss. In 2008, former President Barack Obama stepped onto a slope just as slippery as the glass cliff. Both Obama and Clinton experienced situations closely related to glass cliff as they fulfilled or attempted to fulfill an executive leadership position of our country. We will explore circumstances surrounding their situations.

On the other hand, some women are deprived of opportunities to lead because of their perceived competence and the imminent success.

The Barack Obama Phenomenon

Catherine J. Taylor of Cornell University coined the term occupational minority as a worker who is a numerical rarity in his or her occupation, such as men who are nurses or women who are engineers.[65] This concept differs from the notion of being a token which is typically defined at the workplace level.[66] By contrast, occupational minorities exist at the national level.[67] That being said, occupational minorities are women or minority individuals who are typically denied privilege to certain positions or occupations.

I now introduce to you the term "white savior effect,"[68] the cousin of the glass cliff. Let me explain. The white savior is the deliberate positioning of a white man after a woman or an occupational minority who has "fallen off the cliff." This strategic positioning makes the white man appear to have saved the day.[69] Basically, white male leaders are projected in Western society to perform more successfully than occupational minorities. The "white savior effect" works to promote the notion that women and minorities are not suitable to hold certain positions. The situation fosters a deliberate creation of distrust and diminishes expectations of women and minorities for high-level leadership roles.

65. Catherine J. Taylor. "Occupational Sex Composition and the Gendered Availability of Workplace Support." Gender & Society 24, no. 2 (2010): 189–212. https://doi.org/10.1177/0891243209359912.
66. Oakley, 329.
67. Alison Cook and Christy Glass. "Above the Glass Ceiling: When Are Women and Racial/Ethnic Minorities Promoted to CEO?" Strategic Management Journal 35, no. 7 (2013): 1080–89. https://doi.org/10.1002/smj.2161.
68. Cook and Glass, 1082.
69. Cook and Glass, 1086.

Fast forward to the 2008 election of President Barack Obama. There is no better example of the glass cliff -white savior phenomenon in modern times than this election. Though he was elected by the will of the people as the first African-American president, we all know that the Electoral College ultimately decides who holds that office. Banter among scholars who study the glass cliff-white savior effect postulates that President Obama was most likely expected to fail. This supposition supports the idea that doubts existed about his ability to successfully lead the country during a tumultuous time. He was elected during a time of the largest financial scandals in modern history. The sheets were pulled back on banks, hedge funds, private equity firms, and financial institutions engaging in hideous acts. The economy was tanking, and all heck was breaking loose.

If I were to extrapolate from what scholars suspect, I would surmise that the powers that allowed an occupational minority, President Obama, to be put in this position, did so with the mission to draw on the belief that occupational minorities possess a skill set suitable for calming and nurturing. His skills were thought to be beneficial to pacifying the world and soothing the pain of the American people. As cited in the glass cliff explanation, President Obama was likely perceived to be better equipped to handle crises directly related to social expectations of occupational minorities. President Obama was set up to fail at pulling our country out of the crisis that we were in. Despite the odds, President Obama very successfully fulfilled his duties and responsibilities. No matter his successes, however, he was portrayed as failing at every given opportunity.

The plan was to paint President Obama as the worst president in history so that the "white savior effect" could come into play. After he was supposed to fail miserably, the white savior (a white man) was to come behind him and save the day. This is how we ended up with

The plan was to paint President Obama as the worst president in history so that the "white savior effect" could come into play. President Donald Trump as President. No one expected Donald Trump to be the nominee, not even Donald Trump himself. However, a white man had to assume the role of president after President Obama in order for the "white savior effect" to take place. The next president, the "white savior," had to be a white man, no exception. The ultimate goal continues to be making occupational minorities appear unfit for leadership and white men as superior in leadership roles. This was the goal during the 2016 presidential election, one in which the leadership courage and competence of Hillary Clinton, President Trump's formidable opponent, was overlooked and discarded.

Hillary Clinton Denied the Cliff Experience

Hillary Clinton is an occupational minority because she is a woman. Following the glass cliff-white savior logic, Clinton's presidential bid launched during a political climate in which she could not be allowed to win. The country's transition from President Obama's presidency (one that garnered unjustifiable criticism) to new leadership made for an unsettling political climate. Had we been in a state where the economy and the country were status quo, she probably would have been elected. Because the "white savior" had to be a white man, she could not succeed President Obama. By definition, the white savior has to be white and a man. Clinton was in the right place at the wrong time. As a former First Lady of the United States, U.S. Senator, and Secretary of State, Hillary Clinton shattered many levels of the glass ceiling. There is no doubt she would have demonstrated competence as a president. Due to the glass cliff-white savior thinking, she could not win. That is why she won by votes but was not named president. She won but did not win. She was denied the opportunity to even stand on the cliff. Herein lies yet another example of the cross of challenges that women bear. Challenges are nothing new. In fact, anyone seeking or currently traveling the leadership path should expect them, especially women.

The glass cliff, the white savior, and occupational minorities all reflect the societal perspectives of women and minorities in leadership.

Please do not misunderstand me. Nothing said is meant to dismiss or even minimize what women face. Are the Glass Ceiling and Glass Cliff theories real? Yes. Are they a part of obstacles that we (women leaders) face? Without a doubt. Do those obstacles form challenges that we must encounter and navigate? Absolutely! Despite the accepted perception of doubt and statistics that show underrepresentation of women in executive leadership positions, many of our untold stories are ones in which we continue to break glass ceilings and make firm, progressive steps of success without "falling off of the glass cliff."

Coming to Grips with the Glass Phenomena

The glass cliff, the white savior, and occupational minorities all reflect the societal perspectives of women and minorities in leadership. These ideals represent the unspoken nature of gender bias; classic examples of how male majority rule controls the consciousness of organizational behavior across all facets of leadership. Therefore, the glass cliff is only a problem if we let it be. As women, we should expect challenges in our career paths because we deal with such things as male majority rule, double binds, gender-bias, and a host of other obstacles that exist for the sole purpose of interrupting our ascension to leadership positions. The glass cliff is one of the more calculated interruptions. Understanding the premise behind the Glass Cliff Theory aids in the examination of the interaction between societal perceptions and organizational factors that affect women's attainment of executive roles. It also makes addressing this inequity head on a fairer fight – one in which we first come to grips with the glass ceiling and its kin, the glass cliff. Then we a secure grip in order to break through the glass ceiling and step with firm confidence on top of the glass cliff.

Situations with a looming glass ceiling or slippery glass cliff present challenges for women leaders. Nonetheless, women should be vocal and own the situation that they are walking into, no matter how challenging it may be. This means to speak out loud during the selection process. Make it known that you are fully aware of the current state of affairs. Express your plan to navigate the tumultuous situation, and confidently declare that you will successfully deal with it. The glass cliff should account for female executives' strategic agency in pursuing leadership positions within male-dominated political, social, and corporate environments rather than to simply assume that bias alone shapes their promotion opportunities or lack thereof. This means that women should continue to approach the situation as a means to showcase their leadership and crisis management skills. Do more than acknowledge potential obstacles that accompany the situation. Accept the situation in its entirety. Own it.

Own the process of navigating and conquering challenges of the situation. Know your craft. Research and study to become deeply knowledgeable about the situation you are signing up to lead. Then strategize—not just for the current problematic situation. Evoke your forward thinking. Anticipate levels of change of the situation into account. Take those levels of change into account as well as internal and external forces that may influence the situation. Preparation and confidence in your ability to lead are key to owning and executing the process to conquer.

It is important to understand and confront the challenges created by those who subscribe to the Glass Cliff Theory. Why? Because in order to conquer this enemy you must understand its ammunition! The ammunition of the Glass Cliff Theory is to blatantly put women in positions where the fight is rigged, and the outcome already decided. Current and aspiring leaders equipped with the knowledge of this stealth enemy's existence are better poised to change and control its trajectory. Accepting risky appointments may be theorized as a woman or ethnic minorities' doom, but being equipped with the knowledge of its existence will enable those who accept the challenge to fight this enemy head on! Resist the urge to run from the challenge; just know the fight you are in.

Women such as Hillary Clinton, Phebe Nokovich, and Meg Whitman fight the good fight. They face leadership challenges and navigate barriers in an effort to continue pressing toward the mark. Those of us in this same fight must stand steadfast against the glass ceiling, glass cliff, or any other barrier. We should firmly plant our feet and stand without intimidation. We acknowledge the challenges that we will likely face, not to falter or cower in the face of adversity, but to move forward knowledgeably and nobly. Each of us continues the journey towards our respective marks of leadership success. Optimism and faith strengthen our stance and our steps, as each of us slowly, consistently, and assuredly adds to the momentous wave that has already formed.

Right now, that wave has already started building momentum far out in the ocean. That momentum raises the tide and crashes the shores, but the full impact of the wave is yet to reach landfall. The evolution of a Shero Nation is that wave. Women are making tremendous strides, and crashing the shores, but the ultimate evolution is still building far out at sea. The evolution of a Shero Nation is inevitable, especially with the contribution of each shero who continues to move forward.

Moving Forward

In the next chapter I will define "shero" through a psychological analysis and examine how she fits into the world of today's women. Adding to our discussion, I will bring thought as to how to raise sheroes, build career capital in our girls from birth, and address threats to the shero's progress. This next discussion will add depth and richness to the description of the current rise of the great nation of women.

51

NICOLE ROBERTS JONES
AUTHOR – ENTREPRENEUR - A "BANKROLL YOUR BRILLIANCE" EXPERT - THE CEO OF NRJ ENTERPRISE

My new book, "Find Your Fierce," another God moment, about 10 years ago, I'm watching Beyonce and to be transparent, I'm hating on her just a little bit and what drops in on my spirit is "you know, you have fierce too" and I said "I know this ain't you God, just coming here to tell me I'm fierce." So in my moment I started thinking "what makes Beyonce fierce?' I started deep diving on fierce and here is the thing that many of us don't realize, at least I didn't: Beyonce came up with Sasha Fierce at a time in her career when it was time for her to go into her 'more'. She had been on stage with Destiny's Child and it was time for her to be a solo artist. She knew that was her next level, see god doesn't call us where we are, he calls us for where we have not yet gone. So in that moment she created Sasha Fierce to give herself courage to stand on the stage for the first time by herself. And you'll notice she doesn't even use Sasha Fierce anymore because she sis standing in the full power of who she was purposed to be. So what I know is that if each of us could be unapologetically ALL of us, again, letting go of perceptions and all the stuff we have to get rid of that I had tog et rid off to make the decision to go into my own 'more' in that moment I realized I found my fierce so in that day when I was hating on Beyonce and got dropped in on my spirit I realized this is what I do – I help women find their fierce!

The only reason you need to have this alter-ego, if you will, is because when you are playing bigger than you've ever played before, of course its scary because you've never been there before. Faith doesn't get activated until it is in the face of fear. And so if it is bigger than you can ask or think, then it's going to be scary. Years and years ago, I was on a Mastermind call and Iyanla Vanzant was teaching on that call and she said, and I quote "if you don't feel like you need to pee on yourself sometimes, then you aren't playing big enough" so in order for us to activate that next level, we've got to do it afraid.

Chapter IV

A Shero Defined

I remember a time when I eagerly sought to rise in power in an advertising company that I was working for. During this time (the 1980's), I was not as conscious of the games people play in the workplace. I sat in front of a committee of men who had a hidden agenda. I interviewed for higher-level positions several times, but the jobs were always given to men. It was already decided before I sat in front of them that I was not going to be chosen. Now in hindsight, I see the deliberate social stereotype that kept me as a woman from my desired advancements.

What I have learned is that women seeking to rise to power must understand the asymmetrical relationship between the behavior of two people and how to alter that behavior. This means to tap into your female power and change the dynamic of the situation. If I had been equipped with this knowledge back then, I could have likely had a different outcome. Why, you ask? Because there is power in being female, and when you claim that power and use it to change the behavior of another person, you can change the outcome. If only I had not simply sat there and let those men grill me. Instead, I should have redirected the conversation to where I was in control of the questions asked. We as women do this all the time. Unconsciously, I could have rephrased their questions and answered them on my own terms.

What I have learned is that women seeking to rise to power must understand the asymmetrical relationship between the behavior of two people and how to alter that behavior.

During that time, I did not fully realize my inner, psychological, and intellectual strength. Being unaware, I had not fully evolved into the shero that

I would become. Sure, I walked with confidence and worked to add value in my position, but realizing and acting upon my true potential was yet to come. On the other hand, the shero women of today have mastered the craft of utilizing innate and intellectual abilities to gain leverage of situations. As women, each of us possess similar unique abilities. It is time for us to walk in the truth of who we really are as female leaders. However, the only way we can do that is to realize that we are powerful and destined to rise as sheroes!

Knowing the Shero

It is vital to know the shero. Knowing the essence of a shero gives insight to her potential and ways to help her capitalize on it. In this chapter I define the term "shero" and analyze her psychological profile. This might be particularly helpful for some who question whether or not they are looking at a shero. For you who might be reading this, it might encourage your consideration of what it means to be a shero and evaluation of your individual "shero status." That is perfectly normal. Truthfully, I had to go through this reflective process to understand myself as well as fellow sheroes.

The shero's feminine and "super" human qualities enables her to courageously fight for justice and freedom, often in the face of formidable odds and personal harm or danger.

With a better understanding of who we are as sheroes, I welcome you into discussions about raising sheroes and how to prepare future shero generations to carry the torch for women in leadership. Together, we will also explore threats to the shero evolution, particularly how millennial women are changing the dynamics of sexism and consequently creating objectification buy-in. The objectification buy-in is a concept that requires me to explain the full thought process behind my observation and its adverse effects. The objectification buy-in, its influence on young sheroes, as well as "The Shero Perspective" regarding the discussion as a whole will be presented later in the chapter. First, let us get a clear understanding of what shero means.

---

70. "Shero." Merriam Webster Dictionary. https://www.merriam-webster.com/dictionary/shero.

Defining a Shero

Merriam Webster defines a "shero" as "a woman regarded as a hero."[70] On the other hand, the Urban Dictionary defines a shero as "a woman or man who supports women's rights and respects women's issues."[71] I define a shero as an evolved woman who stands in her own truth, even when it is difficult. She rises to any occasion, changing what she can change, accepting what she cannot, and passing the lessons learned to women coming behind her. She expects more from the next generation than the past.

The shero is the catalyst and cornerstone of the rising Shero Nation. Her evolution impacts that of the nation. The evolution of a Shero Nation is the heroic movement of women who embrace change and use it to empower women so that we no longer expel energy trying so hard to compete with men but instead use that energy to challenge ourselves. In doing so, we create a world that accepts us as we are and respects and recognizes our true and natural strength.

Psychological Profile of a Shero

The shero's feminine and "super" human qualities enables her to courageously fight for justice and freedom, often in the face of formidable odds and personal harm or danger. After researching and conducting ten interviews of modern day sheroes, I realized the following Top 25 Characteristics of a Shero:

- Attentive, active listener
- Charismatic champion for a cause
- Collaborative team player
- Confident
- Courageous
- Discernible follower
- Decisive
- Encouraging
- Fearless leader
- Insightful exhorter
- Inspirational
- Lifelong learner

71. "Shero." The Urban Dictionary. https://www.urbandictionary.com/define.php?term=shero.

- Mission-driven
- Optimistic
- Passionate
- Patient mentor
- Proactive
- Purpose focused
- Resilient
- Respectable character attributes
- Spiritual
- Stylish
- Supportive
- Willing role model
- Wired for victory and success

This list reflects women, past, present, and future profiled as sheroes throughout this book. From Susan B. Anthony to Hillary Clinton, each woman possesses a minimum of ten of these characteristics and is a major influencer in her industry. More power to the shero as she changes the world for women all over the world by leaving her mark in her home, community, city, state, nation and world!

Raising a Shero

The modern-day woman raises a shero by what I call deliberate parenting. I recall raising my children almost on autopilot. I was protective and engaged in their lives. But for the most part, I followed the social roadmap of that day for raising children. My parenting was very attentive and conscious. I protected and nurtured my children by making sure they were fed, keeping them safe, and positioning the right influences around them. On the other hand, what I call deliberate parenting is consciously teaching our children, both boys and girls, how to build social capital. In short, social capital boils down to visibility. Your confidence, poise, and sense of self attracts attention. Your very presence in the arena you revolve in reflects your level of social capital. In business a high degree of social capital contributes to your success allowing you to build a sense of shared values and mutual respect. Boys tend to build higher degrees of this social capital than girls through socialized male versus female activities growing up.

Boys then must be taught that girls exist as powerful godly creations with their own feminine strengths and abilities—not to be judged but to be respected and appreciated. This ingrained respect will not interfere with how boys build social capital but will complement the building of social capital in girls. Our girls must be taught lessons to reach beyond what society imposes, without trying so hard that they lose the feminine gifts that God gave them. Those gifts are powerful. Young sheroes must be taught in such a way that feeds their self-reckoning which will shape and guide their growth. Self-reckoning and the ability to stand firm and speak your mind among your peers will help build social capital. This should be taught from birth. Young sheroes will begin building social capital by being awakened to how and when social capital is built. This capital is formed partially from a process of deliberate, formal teaching and learning, but primarily generated through immersion in the socio-cultural milieu of the early family environment and schooling.[72] Bourdieu concluded that the childhood years were the most important in the formation of habitus and capital.[73] Through observing and listening to those around them, children internalize appropriate ways of behaving and interpreting the world around them, thus acquiring the capital associated with their habitus.[74]

Our girls must be taught lessons to reach beyond what society imposes, without trying so hard that they lose the feminine gifts that God gave them.

Deliberate parenting results in development of sheroes. One person recognized as a deliberate parent is Mr. Richard Williams, the father of Venus and Serena Williams.[75] Mr. Williams deliberately parented his girls because he went to the heart of what his daughters would face with their entrance into the tennis world. He utilized verbal consciousness to make them strong and enable them to take what was going to come against them, including all the racial discrimination. He raised them in such a way that they remain strong, articulate, and able to stand in their own truth. They wear their braids with their hearts on their sleeves. They take punches, and

---

72. Fitzsimmons and Callan.
73. Fitzsimmons and Callan, 355.
74. Fitzsimmons and Callan, 356.
75. Allen St. John. "Is Richard Williams, Serena And Venus's Dad, The Greatest Coach of All Time?" Forbes. Forbes Magazine, January 28, 2017. https://www.forbes.com/sites/allenstjohn/2017/01/28/is-richard-williams-serena-and-venuss-dad-the-greatest-coach-of-all-time/.

in most instances, remain graceful and articulate. They stand strong in the face of blatant discrimination. That was deliberate parenting. I imagine him saying to his daughters, "This is what you're going to face, but I want you to stand strong and take what this world's going to dish out to you and still rise." Those are two sisters who were raised as sheroes. Through deliberate parenting, the Williams family helped Venus and Serena build not only social capital but also life skills that will help them weather the storms of bias and prejudice that they are certain to continue encountering while carrying the torch of leadership in the athletic realm.

A Brief Conversation about Millennials

Like each generation, millennials move, act, and behave in their own unique way. Without a doubt, millennials are making their imprint on society by changing societal norms, which subsequently influences the rise of the Shero Nation.

Statistically Speaking

Millennials differ from previous generations. In their Pew Research article, Kristen Bialik and Richard Fry comment on key distinctions between millennials and other generations:

> Now that the youngest millennials are adults, how do they compare with those who were their age in the generations that came before them? In general, they're better educated – a factor tied to employment and financial well-being – but there is a sharp divide between the economic fortunes of those who have a college education and those who don't.

> Millennials have brought more racial and ethnic diversity to American society. And millennial women, like Generation X women, are more likely to participate in the nation's workforce than prior generations.

> Compared with previous generations, millennials – those ages 22 to 37 in 2018 – are delaying or foregoing marriage and have been somewhat slower in forming their own households. They are also more likely to be living at home with their parents, and for longer stretches.

And millennials are now the second-largest generation in the U.S. electorate (after Baby Boomers), a fact that continues to shape the country's politics given their Democratic leanings when compared with older generations.[76]

Instead of moving out and establishing their own households, millennials take advantage of educational pursuits and opt to stay home longer. They prioritize self establishment, self-improvement, and self-gratification over assuming traditional independence. Their self-absorption alarms outsiders who liken their behavior to narcissism. For individuals concerned about the course of our society, this is of particular concern, especially since millennials are a relatively large population which means their focus and decisions will greatly impact societal norms. The seemingly narcissistic path poses a threat, especially for our millennial sheroes and their ascension with the rising Shero Nation.

Threats to the Shero's Evolution
The Double Edge of Narcissistic Traits

Currently there is an academic debate about millennial trends and narcissism. The Mayo Clinic describes the personality disorder of narcissism as "a mental condition in which people have an inflated sense of their own importance, a deep need for excessive attention and admiration, troubled relationships, and a lack of empathy for others."[77] Current research continues to explore narcissism and its prevalence in the younger generation. The scientific debate regarding millennial ties to narcissism continues. Some researchers claim that millennials possess greater narcissistic traits; whereas, other researchers cite findings that refute those claims.[78] Truthfully, all humans have some narcissistic traits. Research provides no definite correlation between the millennial generation and the personality disorder of narcissism, so we will discuss traits and how channeling them can yield a double edge, one of power or unproductivity.

---

76. Kristen Bialik and Richard Fry. "How Millennials Compare with Prior Generations." Pew Research Center's Social and Demographic Trends Project, February 14, 2019. https://www.pewsocialtrends.org/essay/millennial-life-how-young-adulthood-today-compares-with-prior-generations/.
77. "Narcissistic Personality Disorder." Mayo Clinic. Mayo Foundation for Medical Education and Research, November 18, 2017. https://www.mayoclinic.org/diseases-conditions/narcissistic-personality-disorder/symptoms-causes/syc-20366662.
78. Kira M. Newman. "The Surprisingly Boring Truth about Millennials and Narcissism." Greater Good. The Greater Good Science Center at the University of California, Berkeley, January 17, 2018. https://greatergood.berkeley.edu/article/item/the_surprisingly_boring_truth_about_millennials_and_narcissism.

Take our generation of millennial sheroes, who avail themselves of extended time of living in their parents' home, for example. The question becomes whether or not they truly capitalize on this valuable option. How do they spend extra time at home that might otherwise go towards working to build a life with a significant other or raising children? Will their type of self-absorption later benefit them? The answer is possibly. Sheroes who use extended time in their parents' home as an interval or season to deeply know themselves, reflect on life occurrences, and engage in emotional and financial preparation, will likely leave their parents' home purpose-driven and better equipped to face challenges of the real world. They are more apt to take on and "push through the massive transformations that society periodically undertakes."[79] In this case, focus on self yields powerful and productive results. On the other hand, potential sheroes whose time at home solely invested in their external will likely yield opposite results. Focus on keeping up with the latest fashion trends and hairstyles will only carry women so far on the spectrum of success. Purpose has to be prioritized. Otherwise, this focus without purpose will result in unproductivity, a misuse of fleeting time. Researcher Michael Maccoby, validates this: "Narcissism can turn unproductive when lacking self-knowledge and restraining anchors. Narcissists become unrealistic dreamers."[80]

> *Sheroes who use extended time in their parents' home as an interval or season to deeply know themselves, reflect on life occurrences, and engage in emotional and financial preparation, will likely leave their parents' home purpose-driven and better equipped to face challenges of the real world.*

Millennials are criticized for their level of self-regard and have even been labeled the "narcissistic generation."[81] Whether or not they are a narcissistic generation, millennials are definitely more attuned to themselves and their needs,[82] which can be a double-edge sword. The appropriate focus

79. Michael Maccoby, Michael. "Narcissistic Leaders: The Incredible Pros, the Inevitable Cons." Harvard Business Review, February 1, 2000. https://hbr.org/2004/01/narcissistic-leaders-the-incredible-pros-the-inevitable-cons.
80. Maccoby.
81. Julia Brailovskaia and Hans-Werner Bierhoff. "The Narcissistic Millennial Generation: A Study of Personality Traits and Online Behavior on Facebook." Journal of Adult Development 27, no. 1 (2018): 23–35. https://doi.org/10.1007/s10804-018-9321-1; Niraj Chokshi. "Attention Young People: This Narcissism Study Is All about You." The New York Times. The New York Times, May 15, 2019. https://www.nytimes.com/2019/05/15/science/narcissism-teenagers.html.
82. Rennis, Lesley, Gloria McNamara, Erica Seidel and Yuliya Shneyderman. "Google It!: Urban Community College Students' Use of the Internet to Obtain Self-Care and Personal Health Information." College Student Journal, 49, no. 3 (2015): 414-426.

on self can serve as a catalyst for the development and preparation of sheroes. On the other hand, a misdirected focus can threaten the development of potential sheroes while robbing them of time and energy. Moreover, it can lead them into an even greater threat of objectification buy-in.

Objectification Buy-in and
Its Influence on the Millennial Shero

It is common knowledge that powerful men control what we see on television, what we hear on the radio, and what type of content is allowed on social media. In an attempt to thwart the advancement of women, whether consciously or unconsciously, this faction of male influencers allows and promotes images of women who portray themselves basically as sexual goddesses. Supposedly, their sexuality is their power. Young girls watch and mimic this behavior, thereby not focusing so much on their inner strengths and mental capacities. This distraction takes the attention of the most influential years of a young girl's life and points it toward mediocrity and away from mindsets that promote more positive and meaningful social perceptions of women. The current way of the world devalues women even more and attempts to reinforce society's negative perception of women as sex objects.

Millennials are particularly vulnerable because they are the first generation to have technology with instant, unfiltered information accessible to them from birth. This information starts its impression deposits into the minds of millennials at a very early age and continues throughout young adulthood and beyond. Constant bombardment of information shapes and molds many of their decisions and perceptions. Social media continues turning the page on the effect that history has on where women are right now because history is recreating itself through new eyes. The constant attachment to social media allows unproductive imagery to fill the minds of our millennial sheroes which will, at the very least, distract and redirect their shero energy during the most productive years of their lives. This distraction will result in a negative effect in the short run and will most likely produce habits that will pass down to the next generation. Images with blatant and subtle sexual undertones are everywhere, leading to what I call the objectification buy-in. The objectification buy-in causes us to take a step backwards in our fight to change social attitudes regarding women and leadership ability and suitability.

In the world of social media, all things have become visibly possible. On the plus side, women see themselves and can create images of themselves that reflect how they feel internally. Filters, emojis, avatars, all provide instant ways for women to project their inner beauty. Social media attracts instant attention giving women instant gratification which makes them feel good about themselves. Never in history, at least in my lifetime, have I seen women embrace their differences and love the skin they are in. Small to plus size women are becoming more and more confident and content with accepting themselves as God made them. This is a beautiful thing. Advertisers are moving away from traditional models of beauty and embracing the fact that we are all different and beautiful in our own way.

On the other hand, women tend to go a bit overboard by projecting images that are oftentimes sexually suggestive. These sexually suggestive images, though appealing to the eye, have the effect of promoting female objectification, the very monster that women have fought against for centuries. Objectification buy-in suggests that when women voluntarily contribute to the onslaught of sexually suggestive images, they are potentially promoting the resurgence of societal impressions of women as unsuitable for leadership and more suitable as visual entertainment setting us back to falling into the trap of the Role Congruity and Social Role Theory ideals.

Simply put, accepting, condoning, or participating in these objectifying behaviors, buys into objectifying behaviors and ideals. Women, both young and old, are bombarded with images that follow them in every form of media, television, and music. Smart phones and devices constantly ping enticing users with images that promote sexually alluring images of women. These sexually-charged images set the stage for the objectification of the role of women in society and promote questionable appreciation for their effectiveness as leaders. The promotion of this imagery alters behavior as women co-sign to and mimic these sexually-charged examples.

Some women, particularly young and impressionable women, find it almost impossible not to co-sign to this behavior and mimic the images that they see. Social media adds a new dimension to this buy-in, as it allows women to enjoy the feeling of being center stage and filter their images for that perfect look. This center-stage attention gives them the special feelings that they fantasize about; being and looking like the sexy, beautiful women they see portrayed in the media. It is very enticing and appealing to fulfill their mental impressions of themselves, because in the past, especially, African-American girls had a complex about not being as pretty as Caucasian girls. It soothes a hurt. It is a way for the majority to use blatant objectification and make it look okay. This objectification influences how society will review and form ideals of respect for women, particularly those who buy into these influences.

Objectification is a very powerful tool used against women camouflaged by glamour. Some of the most well-known female social media influencers have tens of millions of followers, most of whom are women. When women buy into this level of objectification, you have to ask yourself where the true expenditure of energy is going. How is this expenditure of energy affecting social norms, and how does it contribute to a change in attitudes towards women? The objectification buy-in creates yet another obstacle to be surmounted. Energy expended on such fruitless activities will act as a headwind in the evolution, slowing progress for as long as it negatively influences behavior.

The Shero Perspective

In addition to defining a shero in this chapter, I also spoke about threats to a shero, challenges to the building of social capital for girls, and the pros and cons of narcissism and objectification. There is a lot here to digest. You may be asking yourself, "With all of these things going on, how can future generations prepare for leadership?" There is no simple answer for sure. However, it starts with the collective. As we stand together, support each other, and defend our freedoms through our political and legal systems, we will see the tide continue to turn. More strategically, we must equip ourselves with the knowledge of the game we are in and how it is being played. Take the blinders off! See challenges for what they are and what they are rooted in. Understanding theories that bind, traps, and threats to the shero's evolution is a firm start. With this knowledge, our judicial shero can begin to enact laws that extinguish many of the laws born from theories that bind. At the very least, offer education such as this book to equip young sheroes with the mindset that has the power to shift attitudes even in the midst of what society professes.

The solution to the objectivity buy-in is simple. Stop looking to the external world for validation of beauty. We are all beautiful, divinely favored, and perfectly imperfect. This is not to imply that external beauty is not important because God also gave us our very own sense of vanity. The key is to join the two forces – your internal strengths and your external beauty creating a force to be reckoned with! We will talk about some of the more well-known women who have done just that in Chapter 5. But remember, we all have the same abilities as these women to find and tap into our own greatness!

We are all beautiful, divinely favored, and perfectly imperfect.

On the positive side, millennials are blurring the lines of traditional gender roles and perceptions of women. Millennial women are more educated than their male counterparts. They are changing how society sees women, especially when it comes to domestic roles. On the not so positive side, millennials take a hard right with sexual provocativeness which is a double-edge sword when it comes to forming a basis for changes in societal perceptions of women.

Millennials hold the keys to the most significant changes expected to happen in the shero evolution within the next 20 years (Walker-Green, 2019).[83] They are bold, uninhibited, driven, and have the power of technological savvy in their back pockets. It is important that we all engage together, support and educate our millennial sheroes so that the effect of the objectification buy-in does not interfere and cause a major paradigm shift within the evolution that may negatively affect our progress.

The Essence of a Shero

Anyone who seeks the essence of women will find their resilience. Resilient thinkers, developers, builders, nurturers, and restorers—that is who we are as women. That is who we are as sheroes. One definition can never fully capture the greatness of sheroes. Our far-reaching worth is ever evolving, even when some have not yet realized who they are as women or their potential as sheroes.

---

83. Barbara L. Walker-Green. "Barriers to Women's Entry for CEO Positions: Is Sponsorship the Answer?" Ann Arbor 1001 (2019): 48106-1346.

Whether or not the shero in each of us has reached her highest potential, we have a responsibility to explore our possibility of greatness at a level hidden by societal norms, a male-dominant society, and in some cases entrapment of our own thinking. Some of us are not aware of barriers such as the unproductivity of narcissistic traits, objectification buy in, or those century-old societal norms. As a result, the potential lying within us remains dormant, thus we need others to come alongside us during this critical development stage. It is the duty of the Shero movement to be deliberate about mentoring the girls and young women of the future to be champions of change for the betterment of all women, particularly those in leadership. This is the chance that our foremothers, the sheroes of the past, fought for before most of us were twinkles in our fathers' eyes.

Moving Forward

In the next chapter I establish a timeline chronicling sheroes of the past, present, and future. This timeline showcases examples of sheroic efforts and accomplishments which contribute to the steady rising Shero Nation. It provides a visual representation of sheroic footprints and strides, including the nation's humble beginnings and incremental steps which led to landmark events, all of which continue to shift and fuel the swelling tides of the Shero Nation.

DARIETH CHISOLM
EMMY AWARD-WINNING TELEVISION PERSONALITY – ENTREPRENEUR - LIFE COACH - AUTHOR

A powerful woman is when we don't allow ourselves to compare ourselves to other women because we take ourselves out of the game and so, to stand in your own power, it means literally standing in it. Owning your own truth, owning your own power, without you looking at someone's lane and comparing. Because we all have our own journey. So if we stay true to what's there, we lessen the opportunity to take ourselves out of the game. I think it's also about really respecting your own desires. What is it you desire? What is it you want in life? In business? In relationships? And who do you show up as? And that changes as we age, because we age, and it changes when circumstances change, but it doesn't mean we don't stay grounded in the true definition of who we are. I think I understand that more so in the last 5 years.

I will say, and I find this fascinating, we all know that within our own energy, we have masculine and feminine energy, right? Men have it, women have it, but sometimes women who have it and are working and showing up powerfully, we rely on the masculine energy because that is what the supportive energy is (for those of us that believe that). Masculine is about doing, support, linear. But when we spend so much time there, we disassociate from the feminine, the intuition, the flow and receptivity and those energies that come to us naturally, we don't always identify those as the business building skills because the masculine has always been in service to that. YET, when we DO, I believe we live a more fulfilled life, in greater abundance because we allow that natural process of intuition and flow and creativity and spirituality – all of those pieces that come in on the feminine side to play a greater role in what we're developing. I'm always fascinated about conversations about masculine and feminine energy and how it plays out in our life and how we associate with it and how we tap into it and use them for what they are: In service to our greater success.

Chapter V

Sheroes: Past, Present, and Future

Why Chronicle this Movement?

There is no doubt that the voice of women resonates throughout the world today! This book will be one of many to deliberately chronicle the history of the rise of sheroes throughout history.

There is no doubt that the voice of women resonates throughout the world today

For women today to fully grasp the responsibility bestowed upon them, each of them must first understand its evolution. "Many are called; few are chosen."[84] The chosen must understand the importance of their role in the evolution and take their place in its progression just as the women that came before them.

For a while, this movement was slow moving forward, but it has picked up momentum as women gained more power over the years. It is like the building up of a tsunami, where the energy accumulates over time before it crashes the shores. The shero evolution is similar to a series of tidal waves. Some crash and die out while new waves take their place with a renewed momentum. This is better labeled as "The Silent Rise." The silent rise to power has been occurring over the past 60 years. Sheroes are now a series

---

84. Matthew 22:14. Unless otherwise noted, all biblical passages referenced employ the King James Version.

of tidal waves, clearly visible, crashing the shores of the world, and growing stronger and stronger with each passing tide.

After years of those waves breaking down resistance, President Jimmy Carter acknowledged the important contributions of past sheroes to the success of our nation. Here is a brief excerpt from the speech he delivered at the first celebration of National Women's History Week on February 28, 1980.

Presidential Message 1980
President Jimmy Carter's message to the nation
designating March 2-8, 1980
as National Women's History Week

From the first settlers who came to our shores, from the first American Indian families who befriended them, men and women have worked together to build this nation. Too often the women were unsung, and sometimes their contributions went unnoticed. But the achievements, leadership, courage, strength, and love of the women who built America was as vital as that of the men whose names we know so well.

As Dr. Gerda Lerner has noted, "Women's History is Women's Right." – It is an essential and indispensable heritage from which we can draw pride, comfort, courage, and long-range vision."

I ask my fellow Americans to recognize this heritage with appropriate activities during National Women's History Week, March 2-8, 1980. I urge libraries, schools, and community organizations to focus their observances on the leaders who struggled for equality – – Susan B. Anthony, Sojourner Truth, Lucy

Stone, Lucretia Mott, Elizabeth Cady Stanton, Harriet Tubman, and Alice Paul.

Understanding the true history of our country will help us to comprehend the need for full equality under the law for all our people.

This goal can be achieved by ratifying the 27th Amendment to the United States Constitution, which states that "Equality of Rights under the Law shall not be denied or abridged by the United States or by any state on account of sex." [85]

---

85. "Why March Is National Women's History Month." National Women's History Alliance, February 11, 2019. https://nationalwomenshistoryalliance.org/womens-history-month/womens-history-month-history/.

It is important to remember the past, so that we can be empowered to fight for a better future.

The war for women empowerment has yet to be won, but we are close.

Timeline of Progression

In this chapter, I showcase a historical timeline of progression chalked full of examples of women who began this movement which contributes to the rise of the Shero Nation. This segment is a critical component of the movement because it contains a living testament to female empowerment and leadership. Each century speaks to the progressive nature of the movement of the proverbial wave that drives it forward.

This segment is a critical component of the movement because it contains a living testament to female empowerment and leadership.

Every generation of females crafted a particular strategy that was appropriate for their "such a time as this."[86] Be it the peaceful nonviolent approach with a strong belief in the system of democracy or the take charge "I AM Woman Hear Me Roar"[87] plan of attack, each method had its place in history. I would be remiss if I did not pay a literary homage to the efforts of the women who came before me. I do this in hope that those who come after me will do likewise.

Where It All Started

Historical documents credit the 1848 Seneca Falls Convention as the impetus for the women's suffrage movement.[88] Under the leadership of Susan B. Anthony and Elizabeth Cady Stanton, suffragists distributed petitions and

---

86. Esther 4:14.
87. Helen Reddy and Ray Burton, "I am Woman," released May 1972, B side on "More than You Can Take," Capitol, vinyl LP.
88. "The Woman Suffrage Movement." National Women's History Museum. Accessed August 11, 2020. https://www.womenshistory.org/resources/general/woman-suffrage-movement; "The Women's Rights Movement, 1848–1920." US House of Representatives: History, Art, and Archives. Accessed August 11, 2020. https://history.house.gov/Exhibitions-and-Publications/WIC/Historical-Essays/No-Lady/Womens-Rights/; "Today in History - July 19." The Library of Congress. Accessed August 11, 2020. https://www.loc.gov/item/today-in-history/july-19?loclr=eatod.

appealed to Congress to pass a constitutional amendment to enfranchise women. The Seneca Falls Convention remains viewed as the meeting that launched discussion regarding women's rights.

During the 20th century leadership of the suffrage movement passed through two organizations, the National American Woman Suffrage Association (NAWSA) and the National Woman's Party (NWP). Due to the joint efforts of the NAWSA and the NWP, the 19th Amendment was finally ratified in 1920. This is the most substantial achievement of women in the Progressive Era.

Historians describe two waves of feminism in history: the first in the 19th century, growing out of the anti-slavery movement, and the second, in the 1960s and 1970s. The following timeline of important events[89] spotlight incremental movements of women's rights and female empowerment.

Historical Timeline of Women in the United States

1700's

"Every great dream begins with a dreamer. Always remember, you have within you the strength, the patience, and the passion to reach for the stars to change the world."

- Harriet Tubman

The 1700's, a critical time in U.S. history, marks time when women began to shed the mask of domestication and see themselves beyond the confines of their homes. At this time potential sheroes mostly exercised their leadership skills inside homes existing under the rule of man. Their worth was not recognized or even respected.

1701 – The first sexually integratevd jury hears cases in Albany, New York.

1769 – The colonies adopt the English system decreeing women cannot own property in their own name or keep their own

---

89. "Detailed Timeline." National Women's History Alliance, October 23, 2018. https://nationalwomenshistoryalliance.org/resources/womens-rights-movement/detailed-timeline/; Susan Milligan. "Stepping Through History." U.S. News & World Report. U.S. News & World Report L.P., January 20, 2017. https://www.usnews.com/news/the-report/articles/2017-01-20/timeline-the-womens-rights-movement-in-the-us.

earnings. American colonies based their laws on the English common law, which was summarized in the Blackstone Commentaries. It said, "By marriage, the husband and wife are one person in the law. The very being and legal existence of the woman is suspended during the marriage, or at least is incorporated into that of her husband under whose wing and protection she performs everything."

1777 – All states pass laws which take away women's right to vote.

1789 – United States Constitution is ratified. The terms "persons," "people" and "electors" are used, allowing the interpretation of those beings to include men and women.

"Aim at a high mark, and you'll hit it. No, not the first time, nor the second time. Maybe not the third. But keep on aiming and keep on shooting, for only practice will make you perfect."

– Annie Oakley

1800's

"If the first woman God ever made was strong enough to turn the world upside down all alone, these together ought to be able to turn it back and get it right side up again"

– Sojourner Truth

A Momentous Time in History

The Seneca Falls Convention of 1848 was the first gathering organized to specifically address a woman's right to vote. To call it historical would be an understatement. It was momentous, and dare I say, paramount. This event depicts the shero posture in the 1800's – subjugated by circumstance but poised with a compelling conviction. Despite potential paralyzing forces surrounding them, the sheroes of Seneca Falls pressed on. Their planning, presenting, and subsequent follow through on the declaration set forth at this convention illustrated the courage and fortitude of women that had not been realized, acknowledged, or even respected. As a precedent to other landmark events that would follow, this convention laid the groundwork for incremental strides of women's rights.

It is true that Frederick Douglas was the only African American invited to Seneca Falls, and no black women were among the hundreds of attendees discussing women's rights.[90] History confirms that it took another 70 years for women's suffrage to be guaranteed by the U.S. Constitution with the ratification of the 19th Amendment resulting in the Declaration of Sentiments and Resolutions, the first document modeled after the Declaration of Independence granting married women the right to own property and that men be held to the same moral standards as women. Although it was decades later when women of color could vote after the Voting Rights Act was passed, the 19th Amendment set into motion the women's suffrage movement—thus, the shero evolution began.

> **1809** – Mary Kies becomes the first woman to receive a patent, for a method of weaving straw with silk.

> **1839** – The first state (Mississippi) grants women the right to hold property in their own names – with permission from their husbands.

> **1848** – At Seneca Falls, New York, 300 women and men sign the Declaration of Sentiments, a plea for the end of discrimination against women in all spheres of society.

> **1855** – In Missouri v. Celia, a slave, a Black woman is declared to be property without a right to defend herself against a master's act of rape.

> **1866** – The 14th Amendment is passed by Congress (ratified by the states in 1868), saying "Representatives shall be apportioned among the several States according to their respective members, counting the whole number of persons in each State, excluding Indians not taxed. . . But when the right to vote . . .is denied to any of the male inhabitants of such State . . . the

90. Swanee Hunt. "Women Got the Vote 100 Years Ago. Now We Have to Get Something Else Right." CNN. Cable News Network, February 28, 2020. https://edition.cnn.com/2019/08/30/opinions/womens-suffrage-anniversary-centennial-hunt/index.html.

basis of representation therein shall be reduced in proportion." It is the first time "citizens" and "voters" are defined as "male" in the Constitution.

1869 – The first woman suffrage law in the U.S. is passed in the territory of Wyoming. Arabella Mansfield is granted admission to practice law in Iowa, making her the first woman lawyer. Ada H. Kepley becomes the first woman in the United States to graduate from law school.

1870 – The 15th Amendment receives final ratification, saying, "The right of citizens of the United States to vote shall not be denied or abridged by the United States or by any State on account of race, color, or previous condition of servitude." By its text, women are not specifically excluded from the vote.

The first sexually integrated grand jury hears cases in Cheyenne, Wyoming. The chief justice stops a motion to prohibit the integration of the jury, stating, "It seems to be eminently proper for women to sit upon grand juries, which will give them the best possible opportunities to aid in suppressing the dens of infamy which curse the country."

1872 – Victoria Claflin Woodhull becomes the first female presidential candidate in the United States, nominated by the National Radical Reformers.

Female federal employees (but not private sector workers) guarantee equal pay for equal work under the law.

Susan B. Anthony casts her first vote to test whether the 14th Amendment would be interpreted broadly to guarantee women the right to vote. She is convicted of "unlawful voting."

Forget conventionalisms; forget what the world thinks of you stepping out of your place; think your best thoughts, speak your best words, work your best works, looking to your own conscience for approval.

– Susan B. Anthony

1873 – The Supreme Court rules that a state has the right to exclude a married woman from practicing law.

1873 – Bradwell v. Illinois, 83 U.S. 130 (1872): The U.S. Supreme Court rules that a state has the right to exclude a married woman (Myra Colby Bradwell) from practicing law.

1875 – Minor v. Happersett, 88 U.S. 162 (1875): The U.S. Supreme Court declares that despite the privileges and immunities clause, a state can prohibit a woman from voting. The court declares women as "persons," but holds that they constitute a "special category of 'nonvoting' citizens."

1879 – Through special Congressional legislation, Belva Lockwood becomes the first woman admitted to try a case before the Supreme Court.

1887 – Susanna Medora Salter becomes the first woman elected mayor of an American town, in Argonia, Kansas.

1890 – The first state (Wyoming) grants women the right to vote in all elections.

"I appeal on behalf of four million of men, women, and children who are chattels in the Southern States of America, Not because they are identical with my race and color, though I am proud of that identity, but because they are men and women. The sum of sixteen hundred millions of dollars is invested in their bones, sinews, and flesh — is this not sufficient reason why all the friends of humanity should not endeavor with all their might and power, to overturn the vile systems of slavery."

- Sarah Parker Remond
(speech she delivered [without notes] in Liverpool in 1859)

1900's

"In the end, anti-black, anti-feminism, and all forms of discrimination are equivalent to the same thing, anti-humanism."

– Shirley Chisholm

The Pivotal Moment in History

Approximately 100 years ago, a pivotal moment in American history took place, the passing of the 19th Amendment. Congress passed the 19th Amendment granting women the right to vote in 1920. This marked a great victory for trail-blazing sheroes of the past and those standing in patient and optimistic wait. There was certainly a turning of women's empowerment tides. It was a pivotal or turning point because it unbridled the voice of women and allowed each one of us more influence in our lives and the lives of others. Women gradually progressed from spectators to active participants. They went from being heard through voices muffled by restraint and resistance to speaking with amplified input expressing the need for more change. The change was slow but progressive. It encapsulates the 20th century as a whole – a time of unprecedented change and unparalleled movement forward caused by the fearless, tireless efforts of our shero predecessors.

1900 – By now, every state has passed legislation modeled after New York's Married

Women's Property Act (1848), granting married women some control over their property and earnings.

1908 – Muller v. State of Oregon, 208 U.S. 412 (1908): The U.S. Supreme Court upholds Oregon's 10-hour workday for women. The win is a two-edged sword: the protective legislation implies that women are physically weak.

1916 – Margaret Sanger tests the validity of New York's anti-contraception law by establishing a clinic in Brooklyn. The most well-known of birth control advocates, she is one of hundreds arrested over a 40-year period for working to establish women's right to control their own bodies.

Jeannette Rankin of Montana is the first woman to be elected to the U.S. House of Representatives.

1918 – Two years after opening a birth control clinic in Brooklyn, Margaret Sanger wins her suit in New York. New York v. Sanger, 222 NY 192, 118 N.E. 637 (Court of Appeals 1917), National Archives, Records of the U.S. Supreme Court, RG 267 (MSDME-CDS C 15:298). Margaret Sanger wins her suit in New York which allows doctors to advise their married patients about birth control for health purposes. The clinic, along with others, becomes Planned Parenthood in 1942.

1920 – The 19th Amendment to the U.S. Constitution is ratified. It declares, "The right of citizens of the United States to vote shall not be denied or abridged by the United States or by any State on account of sex."

Ratification of the 19th Amendment comes about as a result of the 1848 Seneca Falls Convention. But it took over 70 years from the convention before the U.S. Constitution guarantees and ratifies the 19th Amendment resulting in the Declaration of Sentiments and Resolutions, which is the first document modeled after the Declaration of Independence granting married women the right to own property. It also grants that men be held at the same moral standards as women.

1923 – National Woman's Party proposes Constitutional amendment: "Men and women shall have equal rights throughout the United States and in every place subject to its jurisdiction. Congress shall have power to enforce this article by appropriate legislation."

1924 – Radice v. New York, a New York state case, upholds a law that forbade waitresses from working the night shift but made an exception for entertainers and ladies' room attendants.

1925 – American Indian suffrage granted by act of Congress.

1932 – The National Recovery Act forbids more than one family member from holding a government job, resulting in many women losing their jobs.

Hattie Wyatt Caraway of Arkansas becomes the first woman elected to the U.S. Senate.

1933 – Frances Perkins becomes the first female cabinet member as the appointed Secretary of Labor by President Franklin D. Roosevelt.

1936 – United States v. One Package of Japanese Pessaries, 13 F. Supp.334 (E.D.N.Y 1936) aff'd 86 F 2d 737 (2nd Cir. 1936) won judicial approval of medicinal use of birth control.

1937 – The U.S. Supreme Court upholds Washington state's minimum wage laws for women.

1938 – The Fair Labor Standards Act establishes minimum wage without regard to sex.

Black and White Women Unite in 1938

Historically speaking, the evolution of sheroes can probably be traced to a time before slavery. However, the Second Anti-Slavery Convention of American Women in 1838 serves as a glimpse of this evolution. Mary Grew, an abolitionist, of Philadelphia formed the group in an effort to coordinate the work of female anti-slavery societies. At this convention, black and white women met to hear prominent abolitionists speak, while outside, men and boys threw rocks at the building in protest of black and white women meeting together. Prior to the meeting, the mayor made it clear that the meeting should be held and attended by white women only. The women refused; they joined hands, formed a human chain, and stood united against the crowd of men that tried to stop them. The next day, the mob burned down the building where these women met while police and firefighters stood and watched.[91] The mob was exonerated of all charges. Racism was part of the women's suffrage movement from the outset. This is one more incremental stride of the women's movement in the 19th century.

Decades later, women of color were actually given the right to vote through the Voting Rights Act of 1965. The 19th Amendment continued building momentum for the women's suffrage movement, and events such as the Anti-Slavery Convention which was held on May 9 – 1, 1837 were all contributing factors to its success.

> **1947** – In Fay v. New York, 332 U.S. 261 (1947), the U.S. Supreme Court says women are equally qualified with men to serve on juries, but are granted an exemption and may serve, or not, as women choose.

> **1953** – Jerrie Cobb is the first U.S. woman to undergo astronaut testing. NASA cancels the women's program in 1963. It is not until 1983 that an American woman gets sent into space.

"The most common way people give up their power is by thinking they don't have any."

- Alice Walker

> **1961** – In Hoyt v. Florida, 368 U.S. 57 (1961),the U.S. Supreme Court upholds rules adopted by the state of Florida that made it far less likely for women than men to be called for jury service

---

91. Hunt.

on the grounds that a "woman is still regarded as the center of home and family life."

1963 – The Equal Pay Act is passed by Congress, promising equitable wages for the same work, regardless of the race, color, religion, national origin, or sex of the worker.

1964 – Title VII of the Civil Rights Act passes including a prohibition against employment discrimination on the basis of race, color, religion, national origin, or sex.

1965 – Weeks v. Southern Bell, 408 F. 2d. 228 (5th Cir. 1969), marks a major triumph in the fight against restrictive labor laws and company regulations on the hours and conditions of women's work, opening many previously male-only jobs to women. In Griswold v Connecticut, 381 U.S. 479, the Supreme Court overturns one of the last state laws prohibiting the prescription or use of contraceptives by married couples. The Supreme Court establishes the right of married couples to use contraception.

1968 – Executive Order 11246 prohibits sex discrimination by government contractors and requires affirmative action plans for hiring women.

"We need to be as fearless as the women whose stories you have applauded, as committed as the dissidents and the activists you have heard from, as audacious as those who start movements for peace when all seems lost."

– Hillary Clinton

1969 – In Bowe v. Colgate-Palmolive Company, 416 F. 2d 711 (7th Cir.1969), the Seventh Circuit Court of Appeals rules that women meeting the physical requirements can work in many jobs that had been for men only.

California adopts the nation's first "no fault" divorce law, allowing divorce by mutual consent. Wellesley College graduate Hillary Clinton becomes the first student to address the graduating class at commencement.

1971 – In Phillips v. Martin Marietta Corporation, 400 U.S. 542, the U.S. Supreme Court outlaws the practice of private employers refusing to hire women with pre-school children.

In Reed v. Reed, 404 U.S. 71, The U.S. Supreme Court holds unconstitutional a state law (Idaho) establishing automatic preference for males as administrators of wills. This is the first time the court strikes down a law treating men and women differently. The Court finally declares women as "persons," but uses a "reasonableness" test rather than making sex a "suspect classification," analogous to race, under the 14th Amendment.

"Let there be no illusions about the difficulty of forming this kind of a national community. It's tough, difficult, not easy. But a spirit of harmony will survive in America only if each of us remembers that we share a common destiny."

– Barbara Jordan

1972 – Title IX (Public Law 92-318) of the Education Amendments prohibits sex discrimination in all aspects of education programs that receive federal support.

In Eisenstadt v. Baird, 405 U.S. 438, the Supreme Court rules that the right to privacy encompasses an unmarried person's right to use contraceptives.

Juanita Kreps becomes the first woman director of the New York Stock Exchange.

1973 – In Pittsburgh Press v. Pittsburgh Commission on Human Relations, 413 U.S. 376 (1973), The U.S. Supreme Court bans sex-segregated "help wanted" advertising as a violation of Title VII of the Civil Rights Act of 1964 as amended.

In Roe v. Wade, 410 U.S. 113 and Doe v. Bolton, 410 U.S. 179, the U.S. Supreme Court declares that the Constitution protects women's right to terminate an early pregnancy, thus making abortion legal in the U.S.

1974 – Housing discrimination on the basis of sex and credit discrimination against women are outlawed by Congress.

Cleveland Board of Education v. LaFleur, 414 U.S. 632 (1974), determines it is illegal to force pregnant women to take maternity leave on the assumption they are incapable of working in their physical condition.

The Women's Educational Equity Act, drafted by Arlene Horowitz and introduced by Representative Patsy Mink (D-HI), funds the development of nonsexist teaching materials and model programs that encourage full educational opportunities for girls and women.

The Equal Employment Opportunity Commission, the Justice and Labor Departments, and AT&T sign a consent decree banning AT&T's discriminatory practices against women and minorities.

The Supreme Court rules it is illegal to force pregnant women to take maternity leave on the assumption they are incapable of working in their physical condition.

1975 – Taylor v. Louisiana, 419 U.S. 522 (1975), denies states the right to exclude women from juries.

1976 – In General Elec. Co v. Gilbert, 429 U. S. 125 (1976), the Supreme Court upholds women's right to unemployment benefits during the last three months of pregnancy.

In Craig v. Boren, 429 U.S. 190, the U.S. Supreme Court declares unconstitutional a state law permitting 18 to 20-year-old females to drink beer while denying the rights to men of the same age. The Court establishes a new set of standards for reviewing laws that treat men and women differently—an "intermediate" test stricter than the "reasonableness" test for constitutionality in sex discrimination cases.

1978 – The Pregnancy Discrimination Act bans employment discrimination against pregnant women.

"My grandfather was the first feminist in my life. He taught me if a woman can do something, a man will respect her."

– Pam Grier

1980 – Paula Hawkins, a Florida Republican, becomes the first woman to be elected to the U.S. Senate without following her husband or father in the job.

1981 – The U.S. Supreme Court rules that excluding women from the draft is constitutional.

1981 – Kirchberg v. Feenstra, 450 U.S. 455, 459-60, overturns state laws designating a husband "head and master" with unilateral control of property owned jointly with his wife.

Sandra Day O'Connor is appointed by President Ronald Reagan to serve as the first woman on the Supreme Court.

In a break with tradition, Lady Diana Spencer deletes the vow to "obey" her husband as she marries Prince Charles.

1982 – The ERA falls short of ratification.

1983 – Dr. Sally K. Ride becomes the first American woman to be sent into space.

1984 – Geraldine Ferraro becomes the first woman to be nominated as vice president on a major party ticket.

The state of Mississippi belatedly ratifies the 19th Amendment, granting women the right to vote.

In Roberts v. U.S. Jaycees, 468 U.S. 609 (1984), sex discrimination in membership policies of organizations, such as the Jaycees, is forbidden by the Supreme Court, opening many previously all-male organizations (Jaycees, Kiwanis, Rotary, Lions) to women.

Hishon v. King and Spaulding, 467 U.S. 69 (1984): The U.S. Supreme Court rules that law firms may not discriminate on the basis of sex in promoting lawyers to partnership positions.

1985 – EMILY's List is founded with a mission to elect Democratic, pro-abortion rights women to office.

1986 – In Meritor Savings Bank v. Vinson, 477 U.S. 57 (1986), the U.S. Supreme Court holds that a hostile or abusive work environment can prove discrimination based on sex.

1987 – In Johnson v. Santa Clara County, 480 U.S. 616, (1987),the U.S. Supreme Court rules that it is permissible to take sex and race into account in employment decisions even where there is no proven history of discrimination but when evidence of a manifest imbalance exists in the number of women or minorities holding the position in question.

1989 – In Webster v. Reproductive Health Services, 492 U.S. 490 (1989), the Supreme Court affirms the right of states to deny public funding for abortions and to prohibit public hospitals from performing abortions.

1993 – In Harris v. Forklift Systems, Inc., 510 U.S. 17 (1993), the U.S. Supreme Court rules that the victim did not need to show that she suffered physical or serious psychological injury as a result of sexual harassment.

The Family and Medical Leave Act goes into effect.

"The battle for the individual rights of women is one of long standing and none of us should countenance anything which undermines it."

– Eleanor Roosevelt

1994 – Congress adopts the Gender Equity in Education Act to train teachers in gender equity, promote math and science learning by girls, counsel pregnant teens, and prevent sexual harassment.

The Violence Against Women Act funds services for victims of rape and domestic violence, allows women to seek civil rights remedies for gender-related crimes, provides training to increase police and court officials' sensitivity and a national 24-hour hotline for battered women.

1996 – United States v. Virginia, 518 U.S. 515 (1996), affirms that the male-only admissions policy of the state-supported Virginia Military Institute violates the 14th Amendment.

1997 – Elaborating on Title IX, the Supreme Court rules that college athletics programs must actively involve roughly equal numbers of men and women to qualify for federal support.

1998 – Mitsubishi Motor Manufacturing of America agrees to pay $34 million to settle an E.E.O.C. lawsuit contending that hundreds of women were sexually harassed.

In Burlington Industries, Inc. v. Ellerth, 524 U.S. 742 (1998) and Faragher v. City of Boca Raton, 524 U.S. 742 (1998), the Supreme Court balances employee and employer rights. It rules that employers are liable for sexual harassment even in instances when a supervisor's threats are not carried out. But the employer can defend itself by showing that it took steps to prevent or promptly correct any sexually harassing behavior and the employee did not take advantage of available opportunities to stop the behavior or complain of the behavior.

"We must always attempt to lift as we climb."

– Angela Davis

2000's

"We are not born women of color. We become women of color. In order to become women of color, we would need to become fluent in each other's histories, to resist and unlearn an impulse to claim first oppression, most-devastating oppression, one-of-a-kind oppression, defying comparison oppression. We would have to unlearn an impulse that allows mythologies about each other to replace knowing about one another. We would need to cultivate a way of knowing in which we direct our social, cultural, psychic, and spiritually marked attention on each other. We cannot afford to cease yearning for each other's company."

—M. Jacqui Alexander

2000 – CBS Broadcasting agrees to pay $8 million to settle a sex discrimination lawsuit by the E.E.O.C. on behalf of 200 women.

United States v. Morrison, 529 U.S. 598 (2000). The U.S. Supreme Court invalidates those portions of the Violence Against Women Act permitting victims of rape, domestic violence, etc. to sue their attackers in federal court.

The 21st Century

Fast forward into the 21st century. Women have educated themselves and become the highest educated group in the country. They hold top offices, judgeships, and senate seats all across the country. They run multi-million-dollar organizations and will ultimately hold the highest office in the land, the presidency of the United States. This movement has been going on for a very, very long time. Historically, men have fought against it along the way. They have been the powers that be, and will fight to maintain their dominance until the very end. Unfortunately for them, the shero evolution cannot be stopped. Women possess the right to do more than just survive... we have the right to fight for our place in society... From the fight for an equal minimum wage to winning a multi-million-dollar sex discrimination lawsuit, we as women have fought and will continue to fight for equality.

2003 – Nevada Department of Human Resources v. Hibbs 538 U.S. 721 (2003). The Supreme Court rules that states can be sued in federal court for violations of the Family Leave Medical Act.

2005 – Hillary Clinton becomes the first Lady to be elected to public office as a U.S. Senator from New York. Condoleezza Rice becomes the first black female Secretary of State.

Jackson v. Birmingham Board of Education 544 U.S. 167. The Supreme Court rules that Title IX prohibits punishing someone for complaining about sex-based discrimination.

Reauthorization of the Violence Against Women Act. The 2005 reauthorization allocates federal funds to aid victims, provide housing to prevent victims from becoming homeless, ensure victims have access to the justice system, and create intervention programs to assist children who witnessed domestic violence and those at risk of domestic violence.

2006 – The Supreme Court upholds a ban on the "partial-birth" abortion procedure. The Partial-Birth Abortion Ban Act, a federal law passed in 2003, was the first to ban a specific abortion procedure.

"You cannot take your freedoms for granted. Just like generations who have come before you, you have to do your part to preserve and protect those freedoms... you need to be preparing yourself to add your voice to our national conversation."

– Michelle Obama

2007 – Nancy Pelosi becomes the first female speaker of the House.

2008 – Hillary Clinton is the only First Lady to run for president.

2009 – Sonia Sotomayor is nominated as the 111th U.S. Supreme Court Justice. Sotomayor becomes the first Hispanic American and the third woman to serve.

Lily Ledbetter Fair Pay Restoration Act allows victims, usually women, of pay discrimination to file a complaint with the government against their employer within 180 days of their last paycheck.

Hillary Clinton becomes Secretary of State on January 21, 2009. She is the third woman in U.S. history to hold this position. After four years, she stepped down.

2010 – The Affordable Health Care Act is signed into law. Under this law, private health insurance companies must provide birth control without copays or deductibles. The law requires private insurance companies to cover preventive services.

Elena Kagan is confirmed to the Supreme Court of the United States; Kagan is the fourth female to serve on the Supreme Court.

2013 – The ban against women in military combat positions is removed; this overturned a1994 Pentagon decision restricting women from combat roles.

Reauthorization of the Violence Against Women Act. The new bill extends coverage to women of Native American tribal lands who are attacked by non-tribal residents, as well as lesbians and immigrants.

In United States v. Windsor 570, the U.S. Supreme Court decides that a key part of DOMA, the law that restricts federal recognition of same-sex marriage, is unconstitutional because it violates the equal protection clause of the constitution.

The ban against women in military combat positions is removed, overturning a 1994 Pentagon decision that restricted women from combat roles.

2016 – Hillary Rodham Clinton secures the Democratic presidential nomination, becoming the first U.S. woman to lead the ticket of a major party. She loses to Republican Donald Trump in the fall.

The Supreme Court strikes down onerous abortion clinic regulations that were forcing women's clinics to close.

2017 – Congress has a record number of women, with 104 female House members and 21 female Senators, including the chamber's first Latina, Nevada Sen. Catherine Cortez Masto.

2017 Women's March

January 21, 2017 marks the largest protest in U.S. history. Millions of women across the country and women from 60 other countries actually joined the resistance. This protest embraced the full spectrum of American women. The goal was to stand in solidarity and fight for women's rights.

"One isn't necessarily born with courage, but one is born with potential. Without courage, we cannot practice any other virtue with consistency. We can't be kind, true, merciful, generous, or honest."

– Maya Angelou

2019 – Harris County, Texas elects 19 African-American women as judges.

As we mentioned earlier, there has been a consistent silent building of the tidal wave in the process of reshaping the face of this nation's leadership. 2019 was an exceptional year for a group of women in Harris County, Texas, 19 African-American women were elected judges. This is especially unusual because Houston, though one of the most culturally diverse cities in the nation, has often not reflected that in its justice system leadership. That all changed as a result of straight ticket voting. Senate candidate Beto O'Rourke lost the election to Republican Ted Cruz, but he carried Harris County by 17 points.

2019 was an exceptional year for a group of women in Harris County, Texas, The women who are currently in judgeships in Harris County include Judge Shannon Baldwin, Judge Lucia Bates, Judge Ronnisha Bowman, Judge Sharon M. Burney, Judge Dedra Davis, Judge Linda Marie Dunson, Judge Toria J. Finch, Judge Ramona Franklin, Judge Lori Chambers Gray, Judge Angela Graves-Harrington, Judge Cassandra Y. Holleman, Judge Erica Hughes, Judge Maria T. Jackson, Judge Tonya Jones, Judge Latosha Lewis Payne, Judge Michelle Moore, Judge Sandra Peake, Judge Germaine Tanner and Judge LaShawn A. Williams.[92]

2020 – The first African-American woman named as vice presidential nominee.

As of this very moment in the writing of this book, August 11, 2020, Joe Biden, the presumptive Democratic nominee names the first African-American woman in history as his vice-presidential running mate. If this is not indisputable proof of the inevitable rise of the Shero Nation, nothing is!

Mrs. Kamala Harris, born October 20, 1964 is an American lawyer and politician serving as the junior United States Senator from California since 2017. Born to a Jamaican father and Indian mother, the 55-year-old first-term senator is one of the party's most prominent figures. She quickly became a top contender for the No. 2 spot after her own White House campaign ended. In a tweet, Biden called Harris a "fearless fighter for the little guy, and one of the country's finest public servants."

A member of the Democratic Party, Harris is the second African-American woman and the first South Asian American to serve in the United States Senate.[93]

Kamala Harris' vice-presidential nomination is not only an accomplishment for her, but it serves as a landmark event for the shero movement! It is undoubtedly a shero stride of 2020. Those of us standing to witness this historical event do so with gratitude for those who paved the way for her. Moreover, we watch with pure elation as she rises to compete for a noteworthy position in our country.

Through all of the joy and proudness felt on this day, still male group-think rears its ugly head as President Trump tweets, "Some people would say that men are insulted by that. And some people would say it's fine. I don't know."

Although male group think is still very prevalent, we will not be stopped! This nation of sheroes stand to congratulate and support our sister, Kamala Harris! We stand in solidarity with her as she embarks upon her new, very challenging journey. Introducing our new slogan, "Now sheroes, we rise!"

92. Andrew Schneider. "Meet 'Black Girl Magic,' The 19 African-American Women Elected as Judges in Texas." NPR. NPR, January 16, 2019. https://www.npr.org/2019/01/16/685815783/meet-black-girl-magic-the-19-african-american-women-elected-as-judges-in-texas.

93. Kathleen Ronayne, and Will Weissert. "Biden Picks Kamala Harris as Running Mate, First Black Woman." AP NEWS. Associated Press, August 11, 2020. https://apnews.com/905fa6cee7441c8b0cd5363d578278ce.

A Special Note

History has proven that empowered women will fight to change unfair situations that plague and hinder their forward motion. Studies suggest that female leaders have a behavioral repertoire that includes more communal features than their male counterparts.[94] As a result, women receive disapproving and uncooperative reactions more often than men when they act in an assertive or direct manner.[95] But, women-centered leadership also has positive effects in times of crisis. This is evident in the midst of the COVID-19 Pandemic. It is imperative that we address the difference in results (number of cases and deaths) and the handling of the pandemic between female-led nations versus male-led nations during COVID-19 and the striking revelation that has become a main point of discussion in 2020.

History has proven that empowered women will fight to change unfair situations that plague and hinder their forward motion.

Male Versus Female-Led Nations and the Pandemic

Crisis is a true litmus test for leaders, both men and women. The pandemic has tried and tested the great leaders of the world like no other 21st century malady. Stereotypical female qualities based on innate emotional sensitivity and physiological differences may give men pause, but women are also known to have stronger interpersonal skills and a collaborative leadership style. There are inherent qualities that come with the authentic feminine mystique. According to Chamorro-Premuzic and Wittenberg-Cox, "Countries with women in leadership have suffered six times fewer confirmed deaths from Covid-19 than countries with governments led by men. Unsurprisingly, the media has swelled with stories of their pragmatism, prowess

The pandemic has tried and tested the great leaders of the world like no other 21st century malady.

---

94. Eagly and Karau, 590.
95. Eagly and Karau, 591.
96. Tomas Chamorro-Premuzic and Avivah Wittenberg-Cox. "Will the Pandemic Reshape Notions of Female Leadership?" Harvard Business Review, June 26, 2020. https://hbr.org/2020/06/will-the-pandemic-reshape-notions-of-female-leadership.

— and humanity."[96] Female leaders in places like New Zealand, Taiwan, Iceland, have all been applauded for their effective strategies in combating the virus.[97] Their success has led to wider conversations regarding male versus female leadership style. The pandemic brought visibility to the strong, powerful, and efficient wiring of women and their effective management of crisis situations. In fact, their leadership strength and skillful crisis management abilities are coming to the forefront in the face of nations around the world. The progress of women cannot be denied. The title of Garner's article (2020) poses a poignant question: "Female Leadership During COVID-19: What Can We Learn?"[98] Experts argue that any leader can be successful, if he or she is able to demonstrate a balance of strength and compassion. For women, strength and compassion are natural talents. Shelly Zalis provides the perfect conclusion to this discussion:

Perhaps COVID-19 has shown the world what should have been obvious all along: The qualities that make women excellent caregivers are also what make them great leaders. "I don't see any contradiction in being empathetic and compassionate and being a strong leader. That's not weakness. That's strength," said Ellen Johnson Sirleaf, former president of Liberia and recipient of the Nobel Peace Prize. She knows a thing or two about leading through a crisis, as she navigated Liberia through the Ebola virus outbreak of 2014. It feels fitting to conclude with her words, which I echo wholeheartedly: "The power of women has not yet been fully tested or tapped. We need to build towards using it more often.[99]

Men and women may have different leadership styles, but they can complement each other. Think about it. Men and women alike demonstrate their abilities to lead. More recently, women have proven their leadership competence on an international level. If women are given the opportunity to work with men as equals, everyone will benefit from what this teamwork will produce. But first, we must continue to rise, right persistent wrongs, and prepare all sheroes to stand and take their rightful place in the Shero Nation.

97. Rob Dube. "Compassionate Leadership Can Create a Better Economy and a Happier World." Forbes. Forbes Magazine, August 3, 2020. https://www.forbes.com/sites/robdube/2020/08/03/compassionate-leadership-can-create-a-better-economy-and-a-happier-world/.
98. Bethany Garner. "Female Leadership During COVID-19: What Can We Learn?" Business Because. Business Because, Ltd, June 19, 2020. https://www.businessbecause.com/news/insights/7028/learn-female-leadership-covid-19.
99. Shelley Zalis. "In the COVID-19 Era, Female Leaders Are Shining - Here's Why." NBC News. NBCUniversal News Group, June 9, 2020. https://www.nbcnews.com/know-your-value/feature/covid-19-era-female-leaders-are-shining-here-s-why-ncna1227931.

Past, Present, and Future Sheroes

Numerous obstacles which hinder our growth and acceleration in power and leadership positions have existed since the beginning of time. Nevertheless, we rise. Sheroes of the past rose despite the pressure of going against societal norms and, in some cases, impending danger. They made consistent progressive steps resulting in the turning point in women's rights. Sheroes of the present capitalize on efforts of the past. In addition to maintaining roles as loving and nurturing mothers and wives, we have risen to distinguished positions such as respected athletes, entrepreneurs, elected judges, CEO's of Fortune 500 companies, presidential and vice-presidential nominees, and even competent leaders on an international level.

Sheroes of the future must continue the progression by taking our focus away from what is in the way of our advancement and concentrating on building a better nation, a Shero Nation. Remove the need to be a part of the "boys club," and not worry about fitting in or what someone thinks about our leadership style; just do us. Of course, we are going to receive a lot of criticism from men because we are standing in our own truth, but it is worth it. Taking this stance will be a challenge, and it is going to take a while for society to adjust, but they will because they will have no choice. Remember, the shero evolution and rise of our nation is inevitable!

Sheroes of the future must continue the progression by taking our focus away from what is in the way of our advancement and concentrating on building a better nation, a Shero Nation.

Moving Forward

The next chapter, Asunder, brings describe the emergence of the Shero Nation, its timeline posturing, and the inevitability of its rise. The rise of a Shero Nation is not a takeover but a taking of what we are capable of building. It is a shared existence with the world as an evolutionary and unstoppable phenomenon.

JOAN MONTREUIL
AUTHOR – FILMMAKER - OWNER, BRILLIANT WOMEN IN FILM AND WISDOM PRODUCTIONS

I am a mother, wife, sister, daughter, mentor, friend and also an author and filmmaker. My calling is to encourage women and to empower them to be the best that they can be. It is my goal to make sure I pay it forward!

Why Film? I really didn't know how far I was going to go until I started writing a book. When I started the book, I said I need to make sure that my voice represents all the experiences I've had. So when I wrote the first book, I turned the first book into a movie which was "Walk by Faith" (2014). I wanted to grab a larger audience, so I turned to film. Once I started getting into the film world, I loved it and have been here ever since. I have received the support that I needed to be a great filmmaker. It's more than just God calling you to do it, when He calls you, He also sends the support you need. That's why I love film! I think I'll be doing film until the day I depart from this world because you can use it to share multiple messages. Many people won't read, but they will watch a film.

My award-winning movie "Beyond the Vows" (2019) is also about my life. I was going through a tough time with my husband. Adultery became a problem in our marriage. During that, I started journaling about how I was feeling. I wrestled with whether I wanted to do the work to fix things or just leave the marriage all together. Out of this experience came a book, and I used the same process from the previous film to make it available to a larger audience. I turned it into a film because I wanted to make sure that every aspect of my story was told. In film, you can really get the full impact of what happened. I write for myself because it is self-healing. The gift of film making allows me to share my story with the world. My next adventure will be to do a stage play. I want to make sure I master every media and entertainment option. I want to get the message out that there to help other women in adulterous relationships.

Not only is this personal for me, but the bible tells us that the older women should train the younger women, so this is a calling, a mandate on my life. I feel that a lot of women don't know who they are; they don't know their worth; they have low self-esteem, because I was one of them. I didn't know my worth and until I had some elders to mentor me and show me what I was worth; it was so impactful. It became my mission to make sure that other women know what they are worth and that they don't have to settle for less. Every time I empower another woman I am empowering myself; it's liberating for me to do that. Not every woman will be open up about what she is going through, but I see it, I get attracted to what she is going through, and I will try to be of some help to her.

Chapter VI

Asunder

I was born into this world at a time when black people were misguided and oppressed. During my early childhood, I grew up in the basic societal construct for African-American families. The limiting idea that the life of a black person would not amount to much surrounded me. For the most part, I found contentment with that as an ideal because everyone around me looked like me and possessed those same expectations. It was a comfortable existence. Then along came bussing. Suddenly, we traveled to schools far outside of our neighborhoods and encountered people who did not look like us. Many of us became instantly insecure. We were around white people who looked down on us and sat before faculty that did not expect much from us. School became a place that fed our insecurities about our appearances and promoted the expectation that black girls would end up as teenage moms, and black boys would end up either in jail, on drugs, or dead. Soon afterwards, drugs began flooding our neighborhoods, and many of us ended up as expected – dropout teen moms, and our men filled the prisons and graveyards.

By my late teens, a fire sprung up in me that just would not die. I did not understand why, but the harder society tried to discourage me and hold me back, the more I pushed forward with unrelenting strength and determination. The harder the fight, the stronger I became. By the time I was in my early twenties, my expectations for my life had changed drastically. I expected more from myself than I ever thought that I could attain. This process led me to set high goals, even if they seemed impossible. This allowed me to visualize the end result as I proceeded through the difficult process. I did not know at the time, but I was practicing self-actualization. The general

Just as my rise to a place of strength came later in my life, the emergence of the Shero Nation is on its own evolutionary path.

description of self-actualization is "the realization or fulfillment of one's potentialities, especially considered as a drive or need present in everyone." An important addition to this definition is Maslow's hierarchy of needs which he defined as "the highest level of psychological development where the actualization of fullest personal potential is achieved, which occurs only after basic and mental needs have been fulfilled."[100]

Just as my rise to a place of strength came later in my life, the emergence of the Shero Nation is on its own evolutionary path. It makes sense that the rise of the Shero Nation has taken the course that it is on. Before we can get to the most visible place in the shero evolution, we must go through various events in life and recognize the undercurrent of the Divine, that put us in places where our basic mental needs were met. I welcome this evolution, and I am proud to be a part of it!

A Moment of Reflection

The inevitable rise of a Shero Nation is an evolutionary buildup of situations, activities, and social perceptual shifts all lining up and forcing a change in the patterns, behaviors, and attitudes in society. As we continue to fight for equality, each generation realizes successes that we pay forward to the next generation. The ultimate prize of recognizing the shero within us will ultimately release us from the theories that bind, us. What a wonderful prize! As sheroes we stand in our own truth and own our femininity. We harness our feminine power in ways that motivate and influence people, leaving those around us with no choice but to acknowledge and respect our presence. This rise in power is evolutionary as opposed to revolutionary, and it is happening as we speak.

The power of the evolution of women to their place in positions of power owes its origin to historical battles including enslavement, subservantism, and deliberate attacks against our self-esteem including physical

---

100. Maslow, Abraham. H. (1943). "A Theory of Human Motivation." Psychological Review, 50, (1943): 370–396.

abuse. As our sisters of the past fought and endured these situations, they grew stronger and more determined. Countless strides were made but much under the strict "supervision" of men. With divine favor, we became stronger, more educated and gained the respectful attention of men, yet we continue to face social stigmas and gender bias. Forging through, we began to use education as a catapult into higher echelons of power in the corporate and political worlds. The support of our sisters, increased independence through the accumulation of wealth, some male support, and legal changes helped widen the lanes allowing more and more of us to come into our own.

Forward movement over previous years foreshadows a greater movement, one that will transform the landscape for women. It is none other than the shero evolution. This chapter describes the forces including the great wealth transfer, education, community and other supportive entities behind the shero evolution and what makes it truly unstoppable! The churning evolution precedes the rise of the Shero Nation. This nation confronts adversity and proclaims that nothing or no one will separate it from its emergence and final establishment. No one or nothing can or will stop this movement.

Asunder

"Asunder" is an intransitive verb which means to become broken into parts or disunited. In this chapter, I speak to the strength of the shero evolution and the fact that no man can tear it apart. Notwithstanding, we will also discuss internal and external threats to the evolution – threats that could possibly damage or hinder its forward motion. We explore the law as an external factor and delve into a discussion of how some millennial behaviors may be an opposing force and what millennials can do to recognize and abort opposing behaviors.

Asunder speaks to menacing and even hostile forces that challenge evolutionary steps and efforts leading up to the imminent rise of our great nation. Asunder loomed when women had no other choice but to succumb as property to their husbands or fathers. Its rancorous presence was felt when men opposed the 1938 uniting efforts of black and white women, by hurling rocks at their meeting location and eventually burning down that same building. Asunder stood comfortably as authorities hired to protect and serve stood by and watched those men commit the crime. It punctuated its presence by seeing to it that those same men were not punished for that crime. Nevertheless, asunder did not prevail back then, and it will not make a comeback now. Asunder now stands dwarfed to the stature of our rising nation.

The inevitable rise of our great Shero Nation can be likened to the evolution of technology. It is planned, rooted in a need for advancement, and once it arrives, there is no changing it. There is no going back. The evolution of the Shero Nation is the coming together of women and their innate power as nurturers and leaders. We use these innate divine gifts in our rise to power. This powerful movement is imminent and as definite as the scripture that declares "...what God has joined together, let no man put asunder."[101] In the case of the Shero Nation's rise, , "...what God has joined together [the elements that support the movement], let no man put asunder."

I assert that God's master plan strategically placed each progressive step of the movement. I further assert that God's divine hand moves to aid in this rise. Anytime I reference asunder or the inevitability of the movement, I acknowledge the power of God as the undercurrent supporting all things relevant to the progress of the shero evolution and rise of the nation. I invite you to think through explanations in this chapter about the power behind the shero evolution and how these powers are in motion and cannot be stopped. Wealth, community, and even raw feminine power are discussed.

One very notable contributing factor to the evolution of the Shero Nation is the massive impending transfer of wealth.

What Fuels the Rise
Wealth Transfer

One very notable contributing factor to the evolution of the Shero Nation is the massive impending transfer of wealth. Referred to as the greatest wealth transfer in history, the aging Baby Boomer population is expected to pass an estimated $30 trillion of wealth to millennial children.[102]

---

101. Mark 10:9.

102. Mark Hall. "The Greatest Wealth Transfer in History: What's Happening and What Are the Implications." Forbes. Forbes Magazine, November 12, 2019. https://www.forbes.com/sites/markhall/2019/11/11/the-greatest-wealth-transfer-in-history-whats-happening-and-what-are-the-implications/.

Women are poised to inherit a sizable share from their spouses and aging parents. This transfer of wealth will put women in a very unique position. We will be able to use this power of financial capital to begin changing the entire dynamic of the corporate world. As the saying goes, "Power is money, and money is power." We will be in position to use this wealth transfer to "buy" social capital! This means the flooding of opportunities to purchase, build, and buy-out businesses which will begin a massive leveling of the playing field in business. With an estimated one-third of the world's wealth under our control, we will become a sizable economic force. Financial strength carries with it the power to control and initiate change. This power, historically privy to men, will change the dynamics of corporate governance that cannot be disjointed. No man can put asunder.

Education

Another influential contributor to the shero evolution is education. As mentioned in earlier chapters, women outnumber men three to one in higher education. The Journal for Blacks in Higher Education consistently documents the fact that in the African-American community, women hold a huge margin for degree completion over men in almost every facet of higher education.[103] They earn two thirds of all bachelors, 70% of all masters and 60% of all doctorates.[104] Education is catapulting the evolution forward as we continue to seek and obtain advanced degrees. Sadly though, even as we become the most educated gender, wage disparity continues to exist. According to the 2018 Census Bureau report, earnings continue to vary greatly between men and women.[105] The median income of a man with a college degree is $74,900. On the other hand, a

Another influential contributor to the shero evolution is education.

103. "African Americans Show a Major Increase in Higher Education Degrees at All Levels, but Black Women Continue to Far Outpace Black Men." The Journal of Blacks in Higher Education, no. 49 (2005): 28. https://doi.org/10.2307/25073292; "Black Women Far Outdistance Black Men in Doctoral Degree Awards: But How Are They Doing Compared to White Women?" The Journal of Blacks in Higher Education, no. 26 (1999): 69. https://doi.org/10.2307/2999163.
104. "Degrees Conferred by Race and Sex." National Center for Education Statistics (NCES): U.S. Department of Education. Accessed August 12, 2020. https://nces.ed.gov/fastfacts/display.asp?id=72.
105. "Income and Poverty in the United States: 2018." The United States Census Bureau, June 26, 2020. https://www.census.gov/library/publications/2019/demo/p60-266.html.

college-educated woman will earn just $51,600.[106] While women make up a majority of college-educated adults, that strength is not reflected in the workforce, where men continue to dominate. This may be true now, but millennial sheroes are starting and running their own businesses in record numbers. As the evolution continues, more and more companies will be owned and run by women. With the impending wealth transfer, not only will we have the educational capital, but we will also have the financial capital! Increased educational capital gives women the upper-hand in leveraging things like technology, engineering, medicine, and a host of other disciplines traditionally dominated by men. Again, no man can deny or take away our knowledge. No man can put asunder.

Building Community and Supporting Sheroes
Community

According to Cambridge dictionary, a community consists of "people who are considered as a unit because of their common interests, social groups, or nationality."[107] Sheroes are all of that and more. Our community of sisters dates back to the Second Anti-Slavery Convention of American Women in 1938. The details of this convention were discussed in Chapter 5. Social organizations formed to promote sisterhood include some *Social organizations formed to* very powerful sororities. Sororities are huge *promote sisterhood including* women's social groups where women do not *some very powerful sororities.* have to be concerned with fitting in with the good old boy clubs or any of the other male-dominated social groups. Sororities produce very strong women through focused socialization strategies, unity, support, and acknowledgment. In the African-American community, popular sororities are Delta Sigma Theta, Alpha Kappa Alpha, Zeta Phi Beta Sorority, and Sigma Gamma Rho. Delta Sigma Theta is one of the largest black sororities, with

---

106. Richard Fry. "U.S. Women near Milestone in the College-Educated Labor Force." Pew Research Center. Pew Research Center, August 7, 2020. https://www.pewresearch.org/fact-tank/2019/06/20/u-s-women-near-milestone-in-the-college-educated-labor-force/.

107. "Community." Cambridge Dictionary: English Dictionary, Translations and Thesaurus. Accessed August 12 2020. https://dictionary.cambridge.org/.

over 220,000 members. Other national sororities that produce our power-ful sisters of diverse backgrounds include Chi Omega, Alpha Chi Omega, Kappa Alpha Theta, and Alpha Epsilon Phi, with Supreme Court Justice Ruth Bader Ginsburg as one of its alumni. The following list is not exhaus-tive, but here I name a few of the many notable sorority alumni:

- *Sadie T. M. Alexander (Delta Sigma Theta) - distinguished attorney; among founders of the National Bar Association*

- *Marian Anderson (Alpha Kappa Alpha) - first Black woman to sing at the Metropolitan Opera*

- *Maya Angelou (Alpha Kappa Alpha) - renowned, award-winning novelist, poet, educator*

- *Nancy Goodman Brinker (Alpha Epsilon Phi) - founder of the Susan G. Komen Foundation for Breast Cancer*

- *Tory Burch (Kappa Alpha Theta) - renowned fashion designer*

- *Barbara Bush (Kappa Alpha Theta) - former First Lady of the United States*

- *Laura Bush (Kappa Alpha Theta) - former First Lady of the United States*

- *Shirley Chisholm (Delta Sigma Theta) - first African-American U.S. Congresswoman, first African-American woman to run as a major party candidate for U.S. president*

- *Lillian Copeland (Alpha Epsilon Phi) - Olympic gold and silver medalist*

- *Aretha Franklin (Delta Sigma Theta) - Legendary and award-winning, singer, songwriter, actress, pianist, and civil rights activist*

- *Melinda Gates (Kappa Alpha Theta) – philanthropist, former general man-ager at Microsoft, and co-founder of the Bill & Melinda Gates Foundation*

- *Elizabeth Glaser (Alpha Epsilon Phi) - AIDS activist, co-founder of The Eliz-abeth Glaser Pediatric*

- *Ruth Bader Ginsburg (Alpha Epsilon Phi) - Supreme Court justice*

- *Kamala Harris (Alpha Kappa Alpha) – Senator, lawyer and first Afri-can-American vice presidential running mate for the Democratic party.*

- *Cathy Hughes (Alpha Kappa Alpha) - radio/TV personality, media mogul, founder of Urban One media conglomerate, first African-American woman to head a publicly-traded corporation*

- *Mae Jemison (Alpha Kappa Alpha) - accomplished physician, engineer, first African-American woman astronaut*
- *Randi Kaye (Alpha Epsilon Phi) - reporter and CNN anchor*

Coretta Scott King (Alpha Kappa Alpha) - Author, civil rights activist

- *Harper Lee (Chi Omega) - Pulitzer Prize-winning author (To Kill a Mockingbird)*
- *Lucy Liu (Chi Omega) - actress ("Charlie's Angels")*
- *Bessie Margolin (Alpha Epsilon Phi) - former U.S. Department of Labor attorney*
- *Mary Ann Mobley (Chi Omega) - former Miss America*
- *Toni Morrison (Alpha Kappa Alpha) - Nobel prize-winning novelist and poet*
- *Agnes Nixon (Alpha Chi Omega) - four-time Daytime Emmy winning TV writer and producer*
- *Stacey Nuveman (Alpha Epsilon Phi) - 2000 Summer Olympics Gold medalist for softball*
- *Michelle Obama (Alpha Kappa Alpha) - former First Lady of the United States*
- *Charlotte Rae (Alpha Epsilon Phi) - actress; ("Diff'rent Strokes," "The Facts of Life")*
- *Judith Resnik (Alpha Epsilon Phi) - second American woman astronaut*
- *Condoleezza Rice (Alpha Chi Omega) - former Secretary of State*
- *Miriam Freund Rosenthal (Alpha Epsilon Phi) - American Jewish civic leader*
- *Victoria Rowell (Sigma Gamma Rho) - award-winning actress*
- *Patricia (Pat) Summitt (Chi Omega) - former American women's college basketball head coach*
- *Sororities have built strong bonds, a sense of female self-actualization and more lawyers, judges, senators, doctors, engineers than any other group association in America! True sheroes have evolved and continue to evolve from these powerful female institutions. The strength of our community bond cannot be broken!*

Support

Any form of encouragement, emotional assistance, and practical help for a specific idea or goal is considered a means of support.[108] Thousands of women's groups aim to support and uplift girls and women. I will name a few of these organizations that represent the shero evolution. These organizations are a powerful source for the grooming and cultivating of current and upcoming sheroes. Some notable female support organizations that play a huge role in the shero evolution include:

- Equality Now - founded in 1992 working to end gender-biased laws in the U.S. and across the world.
- AnitaB.org - founded in 1987 working to put women in a position to excel in the technology field.
- Dress for Success - founded in 2000 with the goal of providing appropriate clothing for women to wear on interviews.
- #BUILTBYGIRLS - encourages girls to use technology to identify and develop solutions for girls worldwide who do not have access to a traditional education.
- White Girl - founded in the early 2000's to give women and girls a voice and teach them the most effective ways to advance gender equality.
- MuslimGirl - formed for Muslim and non-Muslim girls to change the misconceptions surrounding Islam.
- She Should Run - promoting and jumpstarting women political careers.
- Girlgaze - founded by 16-year-old "Blackish" actor Yara Shahidi to push back against cultural projections and traditional gender roles imposed on women and girls from the outside world, media, and culture.

Sororities, community, and support groups form a powerful sisterhood, a necessary aspect of the shero evolution. The bonds that we have as women uplift, encourage, and support the shero movement. Together, we are a force to be reckoned with and will not be torn apart!

---

08. "Support." Cambridge Dictionary: English Dictionary, Translations and Thesaurus. Accessed August 12, 2020. https://dictionary.cambridge.org/.

Mentorship and Sponsorship

During my studies, I conducted an extensive exploration and deep analysis of how mentorship and sponsorship affect women's rise to leadership.[109] I share my findings in the following discussion.

Mentorship and sponsorship are identified as viable defenses against gender-biased challenges for women seeking to reach the upper echelons

Mentorship and sponsorship are identified as viable defenses against gender-biased challenges for women seeking to reach the upper echelons within organizations. within organizations. These relationships have a positive influence on the careers of women who achieve the top positions in organizations. However, one produces more noteworthy results than the other. The following definitions and discussions reveal reasons why sponsorship is more effective than mentorship in a shero's journey to leadership.

Mentorship

Sexton et al. defines mentorship as any person inside or outside of the organization who provides advice, passes on information, or helps someone get acclimated.[110] Similarly, Ibarra et al. defines mentors as providing "psychosocial support" for personal and professional development which can come from different sources.[111] In both cases, a mentor does not actively advocate for the mentee and often lacks the power to improve visibility and advocate for advanced appointments.[112] This leads me to a concluding observation. The following assessment is included in my observation:

> *The author likens mentor and sponsor relationships to that of a parent and coach of a basketball player. The parent (mentor) can encourage, support, give advice, and give feedback to the player. Yet, the mentor is not in the*

109. Walker-Green.
110. Donald W. Sexton, Christy Harris Lemak, and Joyce Anne Wainio. "Career Inflection Points of Women Who Successfully Achieved the Hospital CEO Position." Journal of Healthcare Management 59, no. 5 (2014): 367–84. https://doi.org/10.1097/00115514-201409000-00011.
111. Herminia Ibarra, Nancy M. Carter, and Christine Silva. "Why Men Still Get More Promotions Than Women." Harvard Business Review, September 7, 2010. https://hbr.org/2010/09/why-men-still-get-more-promotions-than-women.
112. Herminia Ibarra, Robin J. Ely, and Deborah M. Kolb. "Women Rising: The Unseen Barriers." Harvard Business Review, September 2013. https://hbr.org/2013/09/women-rising-the-unseen-barriers.

position to promote the player on the team. The coach (sponsor), on the other hand, can position the player for visibility and has direct influence over promotion opportunities to lead the team. Sponsors have a tremendous advantage over mentors as persons with the power to promote or advocate promotion. Sponsorship relationships are vital to making a notable change in the number of female CEO candidates (p.133).[113]

Sponsorship

Sponsorship is defined as a high-ranking person who gets promotions or places a person in visible and developmental assignments.[114] This relationship is a targeted activity that requires action to get the protégé noticed and ultimately promoted.[115] Ibarra et al. defines a sponsorship relationship which includes more than simple feedback. Sponsors advocate, gain visibility, and fight for their protégés to be promoted.[116] Therefore, sponsors are high-profile employees who have the influence to pull people up through the organization.[117] By combining the definitions, I define sponsorship for women as a relationship with a highly-influential person in the organization who is committed to improving the visibility of high-potential women for executive leadership consideration.

In 2013, Catalyst adopted a program called Catalyst Women on Board ™.[118] This sponsorship program matches exceptional female candidates with leading CEOs and board chairs to advance more women into corporate boards in the United States.[119] These sponsors include CEO and board chairs from multiple industries who are committed to improving board diversity by voluntarily mentoring and sponsoring women board candidates. For two years, each participant is paired with a sponsor that prepares and positions him or her for high-visibility within the organization. Catalyst President and CEO Deborah Gillis acknowledges that sponsorship is a simple yet powerful way to accelerate change. Gillis explains the advantage of sponsorship:

113. Walker-Green.
114. Sexton, 378.
115. Sexton, 378.
116. See note 86, 83.
117. See note 86, 83.
118. "Catalyst Names New U.S. Class Members to the Catalyst Women on Board™ Initiative." Catalyst, June 15, 2017. https://www.catalyst.org/media-release/catalyst-names-new-us-class-members-to-the-catalyst-women-on-board-initiative/.
119. "Catalyst Names New U.S. Class Members."

At a certain point, the path to success changes from 'what you know' to 'who you know.' The consistent theme in my own career was people vouching for me and championing me within their networks. And in most cases, one call or message from one of these sponsors 'lending me their credibility' made it possible for me to get in the door, showcase my skills and experience, and land new roles. I wouldn't be a CEO today without sponsorship.[120]

This program, external to any organization, has been successful in the appointment of 145 board appointments to date.[121] Table 1 lists current sponsorship relationships:

Table 1 Sponsorship Relationships of Catalyst Women for Board Sponsorship Programs (Adapted)[122]

Sponsors	Board-Ready Candidates
Dominic Barton, Global Managing Partner, **McKinsey & Company**	**Diane Reyes**, Global Head of Liquidity and Cash Management, **HSBC**
Ursula Burns, Retired Chairman and CEO, **Xerox Corporation**	**Lorraine Martin**, Executive Vice President and Deputy, Rotary and Mission Systems, **Lockheed Martin Corporation**
Mary Cranston, Corporate Director, VISA, **The Chemours Company, MyoKardia**	**Karen Golz**, Former Vice Chair, **Ernst & Young Global Limited**
David Dillon, Retired Chairman, **The Kroger Co.**	**Anne Taylor**, Vice Chairman and Managing Partner, **Deloitte LLP**
Catherine Engelbert, CEO, **Deloitte US**	**Victoria Dolan**, Chief Transformation Officer and Corporate Controller, **Colgate-Palmolive Company**
Michel Landel, Group CEO, **Sodexo**	**Dr. Ilham Kadri**, Senior Vice President and Officer, **Sealed Air Corporation** and President, **Diversey**
Marc Lautenbach, President & CEO, **Pitney Bowes Inc.**	**Marie Gallagher**, Senior Vice President and Controller, **PepsiCo, Inc.**
Terry Lundgren, Executive Chairman and Chairman of the Board, **Macy's Inc.**	**Lori Mitchell-Keller**, Global General Manager, Consumer Industries, **SAP**
Christopher J. Swift, Chairman & CEO, **The Hartford**	**Jacki Kelley**, Chief Operating Officer, **Bloomberg Media**
James S. Turley, Retired Chairman & CEO, **Ernst & Young Global Limited**	**Claire Babineaux-Fontenot**, Former Executive Vice President and Treasurer, **Walmart Stores, Inc.**

120. "Report: 2008 Catalyst Census of Women Corporate Officers and Top Earners of the Fortune 500." Catalyst. Accessed August 13, 2020. https://www.catalyst.org/research/2008-catalyst-census-of-women-corporate-officers-and-top-earners-of-the-fortune-500/.
121. Report: 2008 Catalyst Census.
122. "Catalyst Names New U.S. Class Members."

Mentorship and sponsorship opportunities are vital to the opening of doors for up-and-coming sheroes. At this point in the evolution, opportunities to penetrate the glass ceiling still come at a premium. That premium is paid forward by those in position to leverage their status and extend opportunities to others. The elements of mentorship and sponsorship are additional stabilizers woven into the fabric of the evolution making it unbendable and unbreakable!

Female Icons

Female icons of the past and present give us a glimpse into the world that awaits us as leaders. We have so many female icons today. The list is exhaustive, so I will limit mention to the most familiar. These female icons influence women's growth and provide us with mental and spiritual support. Michelle Obama, Ruth Bader, Maya Angelou, Oprah Winfrey, Tarana Burke, and Sheryl Sandberg are but a few of our shero sisters. Shero Sheryl Sandberg, chief operating officer (COO) *Female icons keep us energized and motivated to continue to stand together.* of Facebook, boldly advocates for women's advancement and supports female growth in professional industries. One of our millennial sheroes deserves mention here: Emma Gonzalez, the 19-year-old who advocated for the survivors of the Parkland High School shooting, demonstrates the boldness and outspokenness of our millennial sheroes. These women come out strong and own their femininity. They walk boldly in a power that will not allow them to bow down to a man or anyone else.

Female icons keep us energized and motivated to continue to stand together. They are more than mere symbols to be admired; they are visual representations of support and inspiration for our evolution.

Male Support

Another catalyst to our movement is male support for women's advancement. Some men speak up for women's advancement. Of course, we have former President Barack Obama. President Obama is big on promoting the achievement of all women in leadership positions, especially African Americans. Then there is United Nations Secretary General, Antonio Guterres. Mr. Guterres is a big advocate for helping to push for gender equality. He calls it "unfinished business of our time."[123] Bill Gates also advocates for women. Men Advocating Real Change (MARC) is a Catalyst initiative that inspires men to leverage their unique opportunity and responsibility to be advocates for equality. The following men are also key players in the movement:

Alexis Ohanian, Founder, Reddit

Antonio Lucio, Global Chief Marketing Officer, Facebook

Bing Chen, Co-founder, Goldhouse

Byron Hurt, Documentary Film Maker and Founding Member, #AskMoreOfHim Movement

Gary Barker, Founder, Promundo, Co-founder, Mentors in Violence Prevention

Jackson Katz, Co-founder, Mentors in Violence Prevention

Jeff Kosseff, Assistant Professor, U.S. Naval Academy

Jeffery Tobias Halter, President, YWomen

Paul Feig, Director, Powderkeg

Simon Ragoonanan, Blogger, Man vs. Pink

Wade Davis, LGBTQIA Inclusion Consultant, NFL

These men acknowledge the blatant inequalities in Western culture and are bold enough to go against the grain, speak out, and offer support to women and our journey to unparalleled greatness. Male support is welcomed and reinforces our bonds by the interweaving of male groupthink into our movement and, over time, changing the attitudes of men as it relates to gender and leadership. This places yet another rung in our ladder making our evolution unstoppable!

---

123. "Gender Equality." United Nations. Accessed August 13, 2020. https://www.un.org/en/sections/issues-depth/gender-equality/.

The Law

You would think that the law would finally "be on our side" and that governing rules would be passed and enforced to close wage gaps and other gender-related disparities in America. It is no surprise that laws designed to "fix" gender disparity in wages, upward mobility, and corporate governance have fallen short. It is also no surprise that laws are either written by or have to be approved by a male majority.

It is no surprise that laws designed to "fix" gender disparity in wages, upward mobility, and corporate governance have fallen short.

In a recent article, Oppenheim (2019) talks about a recent change in the law that affects women's rights to protection from domestic violence. An excerpt from her article reads:

> *Donald Trump's decision to change definitions of domestic violence and sexual assault has rolled back women's rights by half a century, campaigners have warned.*
>
> *The Trump administration quietly changed the definition of both domestic violence and sexual assault back in April, but the move has only just surfaced.*
>
> *The change could have significant repercussions for millions of victims of gender-based violence.*
>
> *The Trump Justice Department's definition only considers physical harm that constitutes a felony or misdemeanor to be domestic violence – meaning other forms of domestic violence such as psychological abuse, coercive control and manipulation no longer fall under the department's definition.[124]*

There are countless cases where the law has provided little support and far from equitable changes as a majority of the legislature continues to be male dominated. But this shortfall in legal remedies has not stopped us. Quite the contrary, the lackadaisical legal support has made us stronger and more forceful than any time in history! We will very soon be in the position

---

124. Maya Oppenheim. "Trump's Decision to Change Domestic Violence and Sexual Assault Definitions 'Roll Women's Rights Back 50 Years'." The Independent. Independent Digital News and Media, February 27, 2019. https://www.independent.co.uk/news/world/americas/trump-domestic-abuse-sexual-assault-definition-womens-rights-justice-department-a8744546.html.

to re-write laws and have the majority voice when it comes to instituting laws that affect us. We will have to gain enormous control in the legal realm to affect the level of change required to re-write many of the male-centric legislation on the books today. With our fortitude and perseverance, we will make this paradigm shift happen. We will not be disjointed.

The Power of Humble Narcissism

Femininity and masculinity are two life forces. One would not exist without the other. Neither is inferior to nor superior to the other. Both are needed to continue life on this earth. Feminine energy is not visible to the naked eye. If asked what is feminine energy, most people would relate feminine energy to outward appearance. Think about Helen of Troy who personified Raw Feminine Power! I state it as a title because of the sheer natural strength it holds. Helen of Troy, the beautiful woman whose beauty sparked the Trojan War, owned a commanding presence that all women have some degree of. All women possess feminine energy. Most suppress it, but it is a powerful natural essence of being female. Female energy combined with humble narcissism is a naturally powerful force that God gave to us women.

Female energy and humble narcissism combined gives its possessor intangible yet immense powers of persuasion.

So, what is a humble narcissism, and why is a humble narcissist powerful? Humble narcissism is defined in the urban dictionary as someone who tempers two contrasting personalities, much like balancing yin and yang.[125] Female energy and humble narcissism combined gives its possessor intangible yet immense powers of persuasion. Women who understand and appreciate this power use a combination of this inner female energy to command attention. We do this consciously or unconsciously, but we all do it to some extent. This is not meant to imply that we use blatant sexual impressions – quite the contrary. It is the raw power of feminine energy. Overt narcissists believe that they are very special and superior, but humble

---

125. Ou, Amy. "The Paradox of the Humble Narcissist Leader." Think Business. National University of Singapore, July 3, 2018. https://thinkbusiness.nus.edu.sg/article/the-paradox-of-the-humble-narcissist-leader/

narcissists know that they are flawed as well. Humble narcissists have high opinions of themselves and enjoy the limelight, but they also know their weaknesses and appreciate the capabilities of other people. Thus, humble narcissists bring the best of both worlds.[126] They have bold vision, but they also willingly acknowledge their weaknesses and learn from their mistakes.

The power of humble narcissism is huge in the 21st Century. The Kardashian sisters are a prime example of the power of humble narcissism. These sisters have perfected the power of feminine energy and humble narcissism and used them to build an empire! Collectively, they have over 10 million female followers, and the numbers grow daily. They continue teaching the world that there is more than one way to skin a cat when building and harnessing female power. Kudos to those sisters!

Millennials are perfecting the use of humble narcissism. With social media as their platform, many millennials use humble narcissism to create social media success stories as influencers and brand ambassadors. Imagine if they were acutely aware of and capitalized on the forces that are actually working for them? They would be an even more fierce and formidable supporter of the shero movement! Millennials currently embody the old saying, "Use what you got to get what you want." However, we must warn them against misconstruing this combination as a means to an end. Recognized female energy and humble narcissism that are channeled and focused can awaken our natural creativity and resolute attitude. Millennials' importance in the relationship to the evolution of sheroes validates that sheroes come in all sizes, shapes, and colors, and they can wield their power using individual and collective strengths – internal, external, or otherwise.

A Shero's Reflection

With time, tenacity, and wherewithal, women have sown the seeds that birth situations where our rise in power and influence is inevitable. The impending wealth transfer, the massive advancements in higher education, community support, and all of the different ways the shero evolution is supported speaks to just how preordained our evolution is. This buildup of female power and

---

126. Ou.

influence will ultimately shift the balance of power between the sexes further, fueling the rise of the Shero Nation. This shift will give us the capability to rewrite laws, change social perceptions, and ultimately force the leveling of the playing field, with the ultimate goal being to co-exist with men in the realm of leadership, influence, and the control of our own destiny.

As women continue building businesses, running for offices, and striving to be leaders in the country and in the world, we will face challenges. These challenges are sometimes blatant attacks against our gender and ability to lead and can be very difficult to endure and overcome. But we are accustomed to enduring challenges and painful situations and still thriving! As the birthers of life, we push through excruciating pain in hope of seeing a beautiful life on the other side of that pain. Being or becoming a shero means to take in stride the challenges that society puts us through, resist discouragement to the point of giving in, and most of all "let no man put asunder."

Despite sheroes moving at different speeds through varying levels and stages of their journeys, The Shero Nation has developed a momentum of its own!

Despite sheroes moving at different speeds through varying levels and stages of their journeys, the Shero Nation has developed a momentum of its own! As more women and advocates rise up in the empowering truth of creating our own wealth and capital, the evolution will continue to mature. The reference to the biblical passage "let no man put asunder" is intended to lift the spirits of those who read this book to a place of divinity as we take our rightful place in society and the world.

Moving Forward

In the final chapter, I introduce you to the woman responsible for past, present, and future risings of our great Shero Nation. This remarkable woman of resilience always remains true to herself while evolving with time to claim her rightful standing. She is all that you imagine her to be, yet so much more of who you think she could become. She is "The Shero Within."

DANIELLE HUGHES
AUTHOR – ENTREPRENEUR - VISION STRATEGIST - FORBES "30 UNDER 30"

A powerful woman to me definitely pays it forward, we didn't get here on our own, someone helped pull us up along the way so I feel it is our duty once we get to a certain plateau or rank, it is our duty to pull others as we climb, that's what life is all about. We stand on the shoulders of giants, no one makes it on their own, to say that someone did is foolish. It literally takes a village. A powerful woman is a humble woman. I truly believe that everything that is here today can be gone tomorrow, so to be mindful of putting too much in money, too much in fame, - all of those things are fleeting, so you need to make sure you have a strong foundation. I always preach to young women that you need to have a solid foundation to stand on because everything can be here today and gone tomorrow. And always make your bed! Those small things will make a difference.

I believe you can build your consistency muscle by doing one small task a day. For me, I barely graduated high school, I graduated with a 1.9 GPA; I went to a community College and then I transferred to Georgia State and ended up graduating from there but while I was there; I decided I wanted better for myself; I know that I can do better, but I'm just not applying myself. So I got obsessed with success. That I would literally study successful people, like what do successful people do each day? Every successful person had a routine. So I gave myself some goals to start small because I didn't to disappoint myself, so I started making my bed. I started praying every night and making my bed every morning. Once I started doing that I got myself into a routine, doing something consistently and that bled into other areas of my life. Now I'm being consistent with budgeting, now I'm being consistent with getting work done or setting goals for the day in my planner. Whatever it was, it didn't matter, it was something I could point to and say "Oh, I did that, I did that."

Chapter VII

The Shero Within

The journey of writing this book brings back memories of where I have been, what I have gone through, and makes it clear where I am headed. It has been my pleasure to share my experiences with you through the words on these pages. In closing, I would like to leave you with insight of how all of the ideas mentioned in this book personally affected me. I hope that you can use the entire discussion as a guide to reflect on the course your life has taken, recognize how silent realities may be influencing your decisions, awaken the shero within, and ultimately take control of your life's narrative. You may even find that many of us have shared similar experiences with the same roots; most prominently, the roots of theories that bind which likely began during childhood.

You may even find that many of us have shared similar experiences with the same roots; most prominently, the roots of theories that bind which likely began during childhood.

The Young Shero's Fuel

As an African-American child, back in the day, I recall living much of my childhood in grayscale – nothing spectacular about it, nothing particularly devastating either until one of the most pivotal moments occurred. My father died suddenly from a heart attack at the age of 42. I was only 12 years old. Mind you, I grew up during a time where the man was the provider, and the woman stayed home and raised the children. When he died, I felt lost. My relationship with my dad was very special as I was his first from my mom's second marriage. Being dark-skinned and bony with very short hair during the 60's made for a vicious time. But my dad always made me feel special. He always told me that I was smart and beautiful, and one day I would show the world just how special I am.

My dad was a very controlling man. What he said was gospel in his house. My dad was naturally talented. I guess he had to be. As the eldest of 13 siblings all born in a small shack in Quitman, Mississippi, he was forced to drop out of school in the sixth grade to help care and provide for his younger siblings. He had to be strong; he had to be the authoritarian figure of 12 younger siblings which I imagined was not easy at all. So, my father was no nonsense! But he had a soft heart for his children, and he taught me so much through his strength. As his first born, he constantly expressed very high expectations of me, much like his dad had for him as the first born. And although I was smack dab in the middle – I have three younger siblings, one who has gone on to be with the Lord, and three older siblings – I was the child groomed to lead.

I remember exactly how my dad made me feel as if it were yesterday. My dad worked for the Santa Fe railroad as a porter, but he always wanted more for himself and for his family. He was in the process of opening Green's Auto Parts when he died. I remember him taking me with him to work at the shop at night after he got home from work. He was in the process of building the shelving and wiring of the building. Although never formally trained, my father was very skilled with electricity, thank God. I remember he wired our garage to ring the doorbell so that we could not sneak into the house at night and come in through the garage door. My older sisters and brothers caught heck trying to do that! I watched him intently. I learned from him intuitively. I soaked up his fuel and grew strong internally but was afraid to show it. As a young girl during that time I was expected to behave like a lady. I played the piano and learned to bow and curtsy.

An Unconscious Shero

With the family breadwinner gone, we all felt lost as a family. My mom, skittish and jumpy, crumbled at his death. She worried how she would care for seven children ranging from 18 to two years of age. When I turned 13 my mom had to find work to supplement her widow's benefit. Back then, many black women were housekeepers. So, she took odd jobs cleaning houses for white families in the all-white community of La Canada, California. I watched her come home every day after undoubtedly long hours of back-breaking work to feed and take care of all of us. It just tore me up inside.

One day she took me to work with her, as she often did. As I sat in the kitchen, I noticed that she got very quiet. I looked and called for her in that big beautiful house with no answer. I found her sitting in a chair asleep. I gazed at her resting face. She was exhausted. At that very moment, I said to her, "That's it. You are not doing this anymore!" She first looked at me as if to say, "Girl please." But something in her made her listen to me. She looked into my little 13-year-old face and said, "But I don't know how to do anything else." "We will figure it out," I reassured her. The next day, we bought a newspaper and looked through the want ads (That is what they were called back then). I spotted a position as a microfilmer at the Broadway Warehouse. The position required that she sit and feed receipts through a film machine that created microfiche. I helped her complete the application. I went with her to the interview, sat in the lobby, and waited. She interviewed and got the job. She worked for that warehouse for many years until the warehouse closed. She then went on to find work with the Bank of America card center in Pasadena where she worked for 20 plus years and retired.

All this occurred while I was growing up. I graduated high school, went to college, and began taking care of myself. By this time, I walked with strength and independence but still unconsciously operated within the expected social guidelines for a woman. As I entered corporate America, I was subjected to prejudice, favoritism, gender bias, and discrimination. I took the opportunities I could get at the time, all of which were "gender appropriate" positions. This was the norm for someone who worked hard for advancement, so I did not challenge the opportunities or circumstances. I unknowingly walked amid a fog of unconsciousness.

Later, I married and had children. My then husband and I sent our children to private schools all of their young lives. I was adamant that they speak articulately and use their words to express their feelings. For some reason, that was very important to me for them. I worked long hours, and my aunt took care of them after school. But one day, after coming home from working hard all day my daughter asked me, "What we gon' eat?" At that moment, I paused and considered all the money that I was paying to educate my kids. When she asked me that question in that way, I told myself that I had to be present to raise my own kids. So, I left corporate America and opened a large daycare facility near our home. That way, I was able to take my children to school, pick them up, and bring them straight home every day. I was in control over the influences in their lives. I successfully ran the largest daycare in Altadena, California until the very month that my son graduated from high school. Afterwards, I sold the daycare and started my private financial practice.

The Shero's Awakening

During this next phase of my life, I experienced the most blatant effects of theories discussed in this book, as well as the awakening of an evolution.

As socialized beings, we all look for continuity in our daily lives to make sense of what we do from birth to death.

As socialized beings, we all look for continuity in our daily lives to make sense of what we do from birth to death. Without some sort of structure, guide, influences, or examples, we would all wander aimlessly. Theories have a place in society to measure whether or not behavior works. When a particular behavior contrasts the natural order, theories arise to challenge and control that behavior and force it into compliance.

Growing up, I was totally bound by Social Role Theory. In our home, girls had different chores than boys. The girls cooked and cleaned, and the boys took out the trash. I witnessed the play of similar roles later in life when the corporate world encouraged women to seek secretarial or clerical positions but supported men in their pursuits to become doctors and lawyers. Social Role Theory validates social thoughts and beliefs that influence the perception of women in society. Our very existence is seen through the glasses of theories, and the cover of theories is a cloud that hangs over as we constantly try to avoid its rain. This rain comes in the form of gender bias, prejudice, discrimination, and doubts about women as leaders and what their role is or should be in society. Again, theories are created and designed to control how we maneuver ourselves within society.

Theories that perceive women to hold a certain place in society existed throughout my evolution but operated in stealth mode in my life. The

Bourdieusian framework explains it well. This framework refers to the physical embodiment of cultural capital, the deeply ingrained habits, skills, and dispositions that we possess due to our life experiences. My life's experiences followed the social norms of the time which conditioned

Theories that perceive women to hold a certain place in society existed throughout my evolution but operated in stealth mode in my life.

girls and boys to accept and follow the social constructs of the time. Unbeknownst to me, these theories played a major role in my decisions and directed the course of my young life.

Part of my evolution that preceded my awakening included experiencing the effects of Role Congruity Theory. For a while, it silently dictated what I sought to become. Right at the beginning of my career, I began to understand that it was almost inconceivable that a woman, especially a black woman, sought to become a doctor or a lawyer. In fact, it was seen as incongruent – or simply put, mutually exclusive ideals – for a female to become a doctor. In my corporate life, I was always considered for positions "suitable for a woman." Since it was the expectation at that time, I did not think any differently. I can now see how that accepted norm held me back from pursuing more male-dominated industries and positions early in my career.

I recall working for the Pasadena Police Department where I was in charge of monitoring the activities of children and constructing a curriculum that would guide their social behaviors for the Boys & Girls Club in Pasadena. The children lived in the inner city and lacked a place to go after school. Short on discipline and parenting, these children were very challenging. I understood the huge task of building relationships and getting them to focus and be still long enough to receive any type of instruction. None of the male employees wanted the position because they did not want to deal with the children, all of whom were black and brown. So, I was offered a "promotion." Lurking behind this "promotion" crept the Glass Cliff Theory and the idea that I, as a woman, was suitable for this particular situation requiring crisis management. Nevertheless, I accepted the task to go in, create a curriculum, and implement it within the club. It was hard; believe me. There were times I felt like quitting, but as I looked into the faces of all the black and brown children, being as undisciplined as they may have been, I refused to give up. The end result may not have been ideal, but I was able to create a sense of unity by introducing activities that spoke their language that they could identify with. Not only did I deal with the challenge head on, but I also made a positive impact on the lives of young people.

Norms of male organizational culture permeated a huge portion of my career. Most companies that I have ever worked for chose a white male figure as the head of most departments. Men made most corporate decisions. Back then the old boy network was very strong and united, and if you were not a white man, you just could not mingle with them. Whenever I exercised leadership ability, I found myself always having to choose between the lesser of two evils – criticized for being too strong or mocked for being too timid. Double binds penetrated most of my early and mid-career.

The goal for sharing my journey is not to reinforce negative experiences, place blame, or even evoke a sense of victimization. I am inquisitive by nature. I ask why until I get to a place where I garner lessons from my experiences. Then, I share what I learned. Thus, my goal for sharing these experiences is to show how they awakened the shero in me. I see now that all of the situations I endured came together to develop my rite of passage. Each event of my life served as a divine time and place for me to go through as I evolved into a shero.

A huge part of my awakening occurred when I realized the fragility of theories that bind. Binding theories are traps intended to make us stumble and hinder our forward motion in our fight to be heard and respected. Whether they are intentional or unintentional does not matter. The true power that exposes the weakness of these binding theories lie within our realization. We must realize that we are only trapped if we allow our minds to believe that we are. While the initial journey of the shero comes from a place of fight, hurt, and manipulation, understand that our predecessors took these painful and necessary steps in order for us to advance. We acknowledge this fact while we look towards the future through our lens of awakening. Because of this awakening, we now redefine what it means to walk our journey as women. We take control of our lives, our minds, our bodies, and the way we present ourselves. We feel strength; we feel loved, and we feel power through our feminine abilities and female energy. By taking these powers to heart and not suppressing them to fit into the male model of leadership, our awakening and evolution will rapidly change our world. We get this from our ability to nurture. There is absolute power in the ability to calm, persuade, and nurture. No trap is strong enough to hold back our liberating awakening and powerful evolution.

The Shero in Me

I realize that I have been divinely favored throughout my journey. I overcame obstacles that I did not even realize were there. Now that I think about it, a unique situation always presented itself within each obstacle I faced. Rather than focusing on the obstacle and its challenge, *I realize that I have been divinely favored throughout my journey.* I approached it as something that just needed to be done. Divine favor brought me through it all. Looking back, I now realize that each experience, opportunity, and level of guidance helped me to gradually find the shero within me. Each obstacle sharpened my skill and will to problem solve. Experiences and opportunities were afforded me at various levels of personal and professional development. Above all, strength instilled in me by my father paid forward in my journey and turned into resilience, determination, and living with purpose. I declare that I am a Shero! I embody the tenacity of my father. I am the daughter who stands by my mother as strongly as the pharaohs who worshiped and respected the Egyptian queens of Egypt. I stand in my truth as the matriarch of my family with honor and respect for my siblings, both older and younger. As a mother, I take full responsibility to be a strong example to my son and daughter. To the world, I take pride in being a woman who believes in the gift that women give to the world. I stand with fellow sheroes as one of the positive examples for sheroes behind us. We owe it to each other to be the best at what we do, be an example to those who look to us for guidance, and always go full on – even when we do not feel like it.

From where I came, where I have been, and where I am going, I know the strength within me emerged from the sheroes before me, and I must embrace a shero's commitment to pay it forward. Even though my eyes were not fully open during much of my journey thus far, I know now that I listened to the right voices in my life, and my experiences led me right to where I am now.

The Shero in You

Not every woman will realize right away that she is destined to be a shero while she evolves into her place. But like that woman, you should travel your individual path with confidence. Rest assured that your past, present, and future experiences will cultivate the shero in you. Therefore, continue to work hard, stand your ground, push through all the obstacles, and support fellow sheroes while pressing forward to get to your destination. When added to the collective shero movement, your individual perseverance strengthens the force of evolutionary tides making an even more formidable force. I take pleasure in knowing that I used my voice to acknowledge and salute the shero in you and the inevitable rise of the Shero Nation. This evolution can be likened to a wave-building momentum far out in the ocean. When it is moving towards land with the pull of gravity and a force only God can stop, it will certainly reach the shores!

I challenge every person who reads this book to search deep within and find yourself in the words on these pages.

I am glad we are joined together as women in this evolution! Let this book be our roadmap, an eye opener, and our epiphany to what is going on right in front of us. As we fully engage in the movement, the momentum will increase. As we engage in our journey, it is best to see the road clearly before us. Let this book be your guide to seeing and facing obstacles with deliberate purpose as you better understand the hurdles that may cause you to stumble.

I challenge every person who reads this book to search deep within and find yourself in the words on these pages. Broaden your view of the challenges we face. Recognize that we (you and our fellow sisters) are destined to overcome and stand in our rightful place in this society and the world. Bring your shero within to the surface! Now sheroes, we rise!

CLAUDIA MACIAS
EDUCATION CONSULTANT – AUTHOR - RADIO HOST - PARTY WITH PURPOSE BUS OWNER/DIRECTOR

My uniqueness comes from growth, from pausing and listening, learning from stories about who my family is and where they came from. One parent is from Mexico and the other is of Mexican decent but born in the US. So growing up and learning how to mesh the cultures and growing up to find a balance where you continue to honor yourself and your heritage. Then you continue to grow and learn that there are so many other cultures and coming together and finding those commonalities, whether they are family, faith, struggles, goals and dreams and I think that's what gives me a pretty unique Latina Shero viewpoint is constantly stopping, observing, embracing but holding on to who you are and you continue to learn and living each day. Also, being a mom and being a springboard for my own girls as my parents were a springboard for me. My dream is to be there for their dreams and goals. And you know how kids get and ignore what parent say but then as you get older you realize "Oh, now I understand what my mom and dad meant". My girls are Tweens, so there is a lot of questioning, but as a teacher and educator, I always say that the best teachers and educators are always constantly learning, there is no finite to learning.

Right now, we have so many necessary changes, like we just celebrated the 4th of July, and growing up we just always celebrated it but when I got to college, I met other people and learned what the 4th meant to them and that opened my eyes to how others experience things. So now it is my job as a parent and educator is to open their eyes to see history and events that have been documented from other points of view. That's what we are seeing now, with all these changes to how we understand situations, for example the specialist in the army who came forward about sexual harassment and the cover ups, what happens to that information and women who speak up about rape and assault. Breaking down systemic racism and institutions. Embracing the fact that our great nation is an infant, or toddler maybe and it is still learning but that there were many, many atrocities that occurred when this nation was built but they were never shared in our stories when we were growing up, as far as in the public school systems, sometimes in our own families we heard about them but now we need to sure 'the good, the bad, and the ugly' is included that way we have a firm understanding of where we each come from. So learning, embracing, listening and doing it with love, we need to get back to doing things with love and humanity as we continue moving forward together.

LENA L KENNEDY
ENTREPRENEUR – ACTIVIST - PHILANTHROPIST

I'm a mother of four children. Two of those are biological children both of whom are married so that makes me a mother of six and I have two wonderful grandchildren. I believe that all that we do, whatever we do, should roll back into family, it should always be a part of why we do the work that we do. So that's why I position myself the way that I do; I want it to impact my family, so that what I do impacts them and everybody else.

I believe that, particularly black people, when we do our businesses, we should consider building that with family, making sure your family is working for you and that they are reaping the financial benefits and don't be afraid that someone is going to say "oh, that's nepotism" but if you look across the country and look at other ethnicities, they take care of their own. I want us to embrace that, to look out for our own immediate family, making sure that if you have your own business that your family is working for you or with you so that you are building economic development and stabilizing ongoing generational wealth.

I've been involved all my life in trying to make a difference, I think our passion comes when we are young. If we could go back, hone in on our childhood and look at "what did I love to do? What was I passionate about? What were the things I was always doing?" When I look back, when was in high school I was on the ASB and I was running for office in school and I found myself advocating and working with people very effectively. Then when I started working in corporate America, I had people who were undergirding me and pushing me and making sure I was constantly being promoted and running departments. So, from all of that, my advocacy from when I was a young girl in high school, my father said to me (we had an earthquake in the 70's) and I asked him "Why did they clean up that part of the city but not this part of the city?" and he said, "well you need to go down to city hall and ask that question to the elected officials." He was pushing me to have a voice for myself, as opposed to me going to daddy and saying, "You do it," he was teaching me how to do it myself. From that point on, it just evolved organically. When I was in corporate America I was advocating the same way, asking where our philanthropic dollars were going, are we giving back to this community? Are we taking from them? So it just rolled over into where I am now. My business is LL Kennedy and Associates and I do consulting work, which is strategic positioning, teaching people in high level roles how to be more effective in their business and personal lives in a strategic way. So I work with people that are very well established and doing phenomenal things, but I just gently guide them to tweak a little bit and it has great impact and outcome.

ABOUT THE AUTHOR

Dr. Barbara Walker-Green holds a Doctorate in Business Management and spent her research years studying social and cultural challenges for women across the world. Barbara's dissertation research inspired her to write about social issues and their underlying causes particularly when it comes to women and their struggles in Western society. Her 20 years of experience as an award-winning financial advisor lends to her ability to identify pain points, reveal them, and be a guide to informed choices. Barbara's debut book, The Inevitable Rise of the Shero Nation, speaks clearly to her skill with identifying pain points, unpacking their origin, and divulging paths for resolutions. This debut book will be followed by a sequence of books relevant to social and cultural discovery and revelation. A native Californian, Barbara currently lives and works in Sugar Land, Texas. She spends most summers traveling the world and meeting new people. She holds true to her family motto "3-deep" whereby she strives to pass a wealth of self-reflection and responsibility to her children, her children's children, and her great-grand-children. Her legacy is also responsible for passing this motto on until generational wealth is realized, each generation responsible for reaching three generations deep. The wealth of family traditions, self-actualization, financial stability, and service to the community is the wealth to be communicated. Barbara is a natural educator dedicated to supporting family and those who look to her for advice with the gifts of wisdom and expertise that she has been blessed with.

CPSIA information can be obtained
at www.ICGtesting.com
Printed in the USA
LVHW090313201120
672010LV00003B/144

9 781735 464220